50 Dramatic Engagers

FOR LEARNING AND PERFORMANCE

50 Dramatic Engagers

FOR LEARNING AND PERFORMANCE

A Guide on Active and Collaborative Strategies Aligned
with the Brain's Natural Way of Learning

Carmen I. White, PhD, RDT/BCT and
Lennie A. Smith, MA, RDT/BCT

authorHOUSE®

AuthorHouse™
1663 Liberty Drive
Bloomington, IN 47403
Phone: 1-800-839-8640
www.authorhouse.com

© 2014 Carmen White. Lennie Smith. All rights reserved.

No part of this book may be reproduced, stored in a retrieval system, or transmitted
by any means without the written permission of the authors.

Published by AuthorHouse   11/05/2014

ISBN: 978-1-4969-4392-7 (sc)
ISBN: 978-1-4969-4391-0 (e)

Library of Congress Control Number: 2014917699

Any people depicted in stock imagery provided by Thinkstock are models,
and such images are being used for illustrative purposes only.
Certain stock imagery © Thinkstock.

This book is printed on acid-free paper.

Because of the dynamic nature of the Internet, any web addresses or links contained in this book may have changed
since publication and may no longer be valid. The views expressed in this work are solely those of the author and do
not necessarily reflect the views of the publisher, and the publisher hereby disclaims any responsibility for them.

Table of Contents

Preface

The key to effective teaching and training is to ensure that participants are motivated to learn and to retain information. Because we have so much content to review in today's performance-packed world, we spend an enormous amount of time lecturing in our classrooms but not giving participants ample opportunity to absorb the information. Therefore, Carmen and Lennie have designed this book to be a ready-to-apply resource of engaging activities that you can use immediately in your classroom and/ or training session.

This book contains creative, practical activities that were specifically designed to engage your learners in utilizing techniques that incorporate whole brain learning. The activities, which can be used for must subjects, are fun and intended to increase academic achievement, improve social and emotional development, increase motivation, and help participants develop communication skills. When participants are engaged, they are more likely to pay attention, learn more of the content, be motivated, and most important, retain the information. Dramatic Solutions' Engagers have the capacity to capture the attention of participants of all ages. A traditional teacher or trainer spends 80% of the time lecturing his/her participants. He/she prepares long lectures or training workshops and does most of the talking leaving participants disengaged. His/her participants rarely receive an opportunity to practice what they learned and are not involved in the lesson. Therefore, most of what is taught is not retained and the learners remain unchanged. Dramatic Solutions' Engagers uses a learner-centered, creative, active, and collaborative approach to actively engage EACH participant by implementing strategies so that the learner's take-in new information, retain more, and apply the knowledge.

Far more than a technical guide, the publication provides an initial overview of whole brain learning theory, creative dramatics, and the underlying science behind learning and cognition. As educators, clinicians, and practitioners, we were eager to share our empirical studies and the resultant methodologies gleaned from our work. Over time, we have formulated 'consumer-specific' methodology for all learners, young and adult learners.

More published content is needed on emerging and evidence-based practices in brain-based learning theory and cognition—particularly regarding exploration of the 'human agency' factor in art and drama-based academic applications. To establish a theoretical framework for our multi-faceted curricula, this manual provides an overview from the literature on creative drama, brain-based learning, and related theories on cognition as well as arts education. In doing so, we highlight the fact that credible research exists to solidify the correlation between neuroscience, creative drama, learning comprehension, and socio-emotional development.

Importantly, "50 Dramatic Engagers for Learning and Performance" delves into common learning styles through the lens of both leading theorists and empirical observations from our own practice experiences. This book also examines the process of cognition in the context of multiple intelligences. We explain how our use of dramatic engagers can not only attract, but also actually stimulate and connect, learners by looking at what the literature reveals—underscored by our own practitioner experience.

(Wenger, 1998) asserts that when we are with a community of practice, we learn certain ways of engaging in action with other people. Our hope is that individuals and organizations will embrace this guidebook and find our work both relatable and viable in terms of replication potential. As educators and clinical practitioners, DSI's corporate principals have specialized in drama-based instruction, learning theory, and cognition for more than 20 years.

At this juncture, we were eager to share highlights from our applied work. We are honored, and frankly relieved, to take this time finally to reflect and 'put pen-to-paper' to illustrate our stories of success, lessons learned, and enlightening experiences. We knew in our heart of hearts that DSI's work was far from ephemeral—but rather had long-lasting results! The compendium of benchmarks overtime served to validate further the integrity of what we do underscoring the necessity to disseminate our body of work.

We envision that our readership will find "Dramatic Engagers" both motivational and inspiring. The book's presentation of instructional material comprises implementation guidelines and recommended methodologies, enlivened by 'real-life' application scenarios. Our interactive approach enhances the reader's ability to grasp DSI's dramatic engagers and infuse them into selected content areas with confidence. Our hope is that you will evolve into a space of transformation much like we came to do. To extend opportunities for others to be engaged is the highest form of being active and present in the moment. It is pure joy. We discovered that it was important for us as educators, trainers, and practitioners of change to take a moment to pause, reflect, and re-examine some of our instructional patterns on both a personal and professional level.

Our personal and professional approach to learning has always had its etiology in the dramatic arts—a path embarked upon 20 years ago and leading to this point in time. Our work led us to places where **dramatic engagers** ended up being the life line not just for the lost learners placed in detention facilities but also for administrators, educators, and counselors who were losing hope and passion for doing the very thing they once loved. We also observed and discovered our work going into places where we did not want to go; we asked questions where we had to become students all over again to our own thoughts and actions. While scary, it was positive to go into the darkness and to come out inspired and ready to move ahead!

The development of this publication allotted us the opportunity to seek more answers, to ask better questions, and to take more risks in the future. As this process of meta-cognition occurred, we found ourselves energized and discovered a space of self- improvement and renewal. There were moments when this was scary and a dark space to work, but ever so worth it—a "found" space that was amazing yet full of hope and understanding.

Therefore, we invite you to come and be enlightened with us. Enjoin in a unique virtual 'learning engagement' and bring the process of human development to life in your organization, school, classroom, place of worship, and community.

The 50 dramatic engagers in this book are creative, active, and collaborative strategies that keep participants lured and help increase the opportunity of moving information into long-term memory across any subject matter or content module.

Remember to enjoy this book since it is SIMPLY ENGAGING!

Acknowledgements

The authors wish to acknowledge the support and assistance of many people in the preparation for this book:

Madeline Darden for her unstinting contributions, as her technical expertise and professionalism during the making of this book were astounding. She also has given both of us limitless patience throughout the process.

Lauren Ransome for her astute and efficient editing.

Mrs. Pat Alexander, Dr. Michelle Bondima, Mrs. Jeanette McCune, and Dr. Antonio Nowell, great cheerleaders, for their encouragement and discussions about how to expand our work.

The late great Patricia Sternberg for her inspiration and for showing us the power in the work with diverse and special populations.

Linwood and Layla for their understanding, support, sense of humor, and most of all good hugs.

Dorothy White for her constant support and technical assistance.

Gregory Hunter for his unique graphic design.

To our friends and colleagues at the North American Drama Therapy Association.

All of our educational family in the Community College Leadership Doctoral Program at Morgan State University.

Lynda Zimmerman and partners from the Creative Arts Team for introducing us to the power of educational drama.

Our clients and students, past and present, who have enriched our experience in creating 'dramatic engagers' for many populations.

All of our family and friends for always being there whenever we needed them, and for encouraging us and allowing us to feel free to be creative, innovative, and spiritual beings.

About the Authors

Carmen White, Ph.D., RDT. /BCT. Speaker, Drama Therapist, Consultant, Trainer, and Coach

Carmen White is a spirited inspirational speaker, drama therapist, and passionate educator who engage audiences worldwide by enlightening the mind and energizing the heart. A leading authority on drama-based training and experiential learning, Carmen is the Founder and President of Dramatic Solutions, Inc. (DSI)—a comprehensive drama education company and clinical practice. Also, an acclaimed actress and choreographer, Carmen embraces creativity as a medium to educate, develop, and nurture talent. She has spent more than 15 years collaborating with government agencies, non-profit organizations, academic institutions, and corporations to facilitate development of their personnel. Predicated upon an underlying framework of creative drama, brain-based learning, and organizational development theories, DSI's interventions include interactive workshops, workforce development training, and Internet-based distance learning curricula. Through DSI and her private practice, Carmen's individualized programming helps to teach individuals and organizations how to 'invent' their future. She maintains an underlying passion for helping culturally diverse teams work together to improve performance, enhance morale, and reach their full potential.

Carmen received her Ph.D. in Curriculum and Instruction and Human Development at the University of Maryland, College Park; a Master of Arts degree in Educational Leadership from New York University; and a Bachelor of Arts degree from New York University in Educational Drama. Carmen is a Kennedy Center Artist-in-residence, certified Process Communication Model Trainer, and Board Certified-Registered Drama Therapist. To contact Carmen about a workshop or keynote address, please call 202-438-7031 or e-mail dramadoctor@verizon.net.

Lennie Smith, M.A., BCT./RDT.
Consultant, Drama Therapist, Trainer, and Coach

Lennie Smith is a seasoned clinician, university professor, and entrepreneur, with over 20 years of experience in public school systems, alternative education programming, corporate and non-profit organizations. Lennie currently serves as the director of a university-based theatre program in Washington, DC and maintains a private practice with a focus on creative drama, curricula development, and clinical interventions. Lennie is a strong advocate for active and collaborative learning in the classroom for disengaged learners. During his tenure as Co-founder and Director of a non-profit drama education organization, Lennie successfully developed and implemented an interactive life skills program at a juvenile detention center, consisting of user-specific curricula and training modalities. Lennie is also a seasoned professional in the theatre circuit, having amassed a prolific body of work in just the past few years alone.

Lennie strongly believes in the power of drama to educate, empower, and enlighten. He is currently a Doctoral Candidate at Morgan State University's Community College Leadership Program. Lennie trained professionally in the Acting Studio at the American Musical and Dramatic Academy (AMDA) in New York City. He holds a Bachelor of Arts degree in Educational Drama and a Master of Arts degree in Interpersonal Communication from New York University. Lennie is a Board-Certified Registered Drama Therapist, with additional credentialing in Process Communication Model Training and Quality Matters Online teaching. To contact Lennie about a workshop or devising curriculum, please call 202-438-6985 or e-mail bdramatic@verizon.net.

FUNCTIONS
for
DRAMATIC ENGAGERS

☑ Content Building
☑ Focus Activity
☑ Social Skills
☑ Problem Solving
☑ Team Building
☑ Communication Skills
☑ Critical Thinking Skills
☑ Energizer

	Content Building	Focus Activity	Social Skills	Problem Solving	Team Building	Communication Skills	Critical Thinking Skills	Energizer
Add-on-Scene		☑	☑				☑	
Add on Story		☑	☑	☑		☑	☑	
All Around the Room	☑	☑	☑					☑
Back-to-Back		☑	☑	☑		☑	☑	
Body Builders		☑	☑	☑	☑		☑	
Brainstorm A-Z	☑		☑			☑		☑
Busy Highway		☑	☑					☑
Character Charades			☑			☑		☑	☑
Commercial	☑	☑	☑			☑	☑	
Content Pantomime	☑	☑	☑			☑		
Countdown		☑	☑	☑				☑
Crossover	☑	☑	☑					
Earthquake		☑	☑					☑
Four Corners			☑					
Fruit Bowl		☑	☑					☑
Give Me Liberty		☑	☑	☑			☑	☑
Grab-N-Go	☑		☑	☑	☑			☑
Guess Who the Leader Is			☑	☑				
Hear My Story, Tell My Story			☑			☑		

Help or Hurt		☑	☑					☑
Human Barometer	☑		☑	☑			☑	
In Good Company		☑	☑	☑	☑		☑	☑
Inner and Outer Circle	☑		☑				☑	
Jack-in-the-Box	☑		☑					
Learner-in-Role	☑		☑	☑				
Living Picture	☑		☑		☑			
Meet and Greet			☑					☑
Meet the Press	☑		☑			☑		
Pair Think-Link-Sync	☑		☑	☑			☑	
Pair-Walk-and-Talk	☑		☑	☑				
Positive Corridor		☑	☑					
Positive Push-Ups		☑	☑					
Review A-Z	☑		☑					
Review Barometer	☑		☑					
Review Toss	☑		☑					
Role on the Board	☑		☑					
Scene Partner	☑		☑					
Spect-O-Gram	☑		☑	☑				
Stand in Line			☑	☑	☑			☑
Star Witness	☑		☑			☑	☑	
Teacher-in-Role	☑		☑			☑	☑	
Team Back-to-Back	☑		☑	☑	☑	☑	☑	
Team Brainstorm Board	☑		☑	☑	☑	☑	☑	
Team Groupings			☑	☑	☑	☑	☑	
Team Story Board			☑		☑			
Team Tapestry			☑		☑			
Team Think-Link-Sync			☑		☑			
Untangle		☑	☑	☑	☑		☑	☑
Word Ball	☑		☑				☑	
Zip, Zap, Zop		☑	☑	☑	☑		☑	☑

Chapter One

Introducing Dramatic Engagers

What are Dramatic Engagers? We are glad that you asked! Dramatic Engagers are strategies that require each participant to be involved in the learning of content. They directly help teachers and trainers increase both attention and participation by focusing on brain-based learning instead of traditional lecturing, which provide opportunities for the brain to process and to retain the information. Participants perform and practice what they learn through active and collaborative activities and creative drama techniques. This makes learning Fun, which helps your learner reflect, recall, and retain the information. Dramatic Solutions' new approach help participants apply what they learn. Keeping participants engaged is the best way for them to gain knowledge. Teachers and trainers using the strategies in this book will be inspired and motivated to use Dramatic Engagers to improve their classroom teaching techniques, while their participants fully grasp the information, making the processing of new data more meaningful and productive. Dramatic Solutions' Engagers are a scientific- and researched-based model. Hundreds of studies on active and collaborative learning show tremendous social and academic gains over traditional teaching and learning.

TOP GENERAL OBJECTIVES FOR DRAMATIC ENGAGERS

a) To break the ice and relieve tension for brain.

b) To stimulate the brain by using as many senses as possible.

c) To prepare the students to learn.

d) To increase safe and positive learner interaction.

e) To protect the dendrites in the brain to increase the processing of new information.

f) To build the sense of fun and pleasure through active engagement.

g) To boost confidence and self-control.

h) To boost morale and teamwork.

i) To build cognitive and critical skills.

j) To increase the opportunity to change and maintain the learner's bright affects.

k) To inform and empower.

l) To reduce threat in the space and foster safety.

m) To practice collaborative and cooperative skill sets.

The idea that good teachers and trainers become great when they allow themselves to learn from their students is more than a cliché. This notion embodies our perspective on the 'teacher-learner' relationship, as well as, the knowledge transfer process. And, perhaps not too surprisingly, as noted earlier in this chapter, 'learning' begets learning. As such, the cognition process (itself a structural element) can be considered an engager as well.

Dramatic engagers utilize emerging trends and best practices in learner engagement and achievement of cognition, which are found throughout the medical, scientific, and academic literature. Some of these interventions and activities include (About.com - Secondary Education, 2014):

Participatory Activities

- Kinesthetic learners would include writing down information that they are to learn.
- Visual learners could create word webs, Venn diagrams, or other visual presentations of information.
- Auditory learners could read a passage aloud from their textbook or from handouts.

Instructional Modalities

- Employing Inclusive Teaching Strategies
- Student Engagement through Active Learning
- Leading Dynamic Discussions
- Utilizing Technology
- Service Learning

The following creative modalities are deployed heavily in our ongoing academic and clinical practice. We have found them to be extremely effective in the participant learner-engagement process.

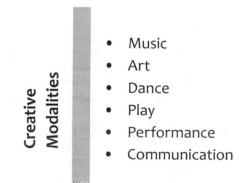

Creative Modalities

- Music
- Art
- Dance
- Play
- Performance
- Communication

When utilizing different teaching modalities, the information is reinforced by all the different senses. In addition, some participants as we will discuss later, prefer one of the modalities over the other. By utilizing different approaches, you have a greater chance of reaching every participant.

ENGAGEMENT WITH THE BRAIN IN MIND

It is almost guaranteed that the following question will arise in the minds of a vast majority of learners, "WHAT'S IN IT FOR ME"? The curiosity may be expressed in many different forms and vary widely from person to person. However, whether stated or unstated, Can YOU answer this opening inquiry? It is a seemingly simplistic, yet huge, underlying question for all of your learners. More important, are you able to provide an answer that acknowledges the multiple learning styles that exist among individuals? In addition, will your response take into account the enormous variations in how the BRAIN processes information?

Recognizing that the brain is an organism within the human body and understanding how this highly capable component (brain) processes information is crucial to tackling the opening question successfully –"What's in it for me"? This realization extends well beyond the answer to the query. Subsequent insights influence how you plan, approach, and assess your entire repertoire of teaching and training experiences.

The human brain is masterfully designed, so much so that most people are unaware of the full extent of its functionality. Short of a researcher or neuroscientist, the average individual simply does not grasp the direct correlation between actual brain functionality and what we do and how we think or, conversely, how brain activity impacts what we <u>do not</u> learn and retain. A pervasive lack of knowledge about the brain's role in cognitive processing has resulted in a vastly underrated view of this awesome human body component. Fortunately, contemporary scientific research provides greater clarity about the multiple aspects of cognition. In addition, the literature is replete with studies that illustrate how the process of learning has EVERYTHING to do with the power embedded in our brains.

Brain-based learning is the application of a meaningful group of principles that represent our understanding of how our brain works in the context of education. When we take time to establish a learning environment that is compatible for brain-based learning, we are giving our learners a chance to engage with strategies that are predicated upon body, mind, and brain anatomy. In other words, by maximizing the capabilities of the brain, we are increasing our chances for real learning to take place.

The Brain-Based Learning Theory similarly echoes these concepts. Perhaps the most important message communicated in this publication is that the brain possesses vast capabilities, which are nurtured through creativity and thrive in sensorial environments. The ingredients in this equation work best when a catalyst (or engager) is applied. For humans, as sentient beings, the more exposure the brain receives, the more robust the development of this organism's inner mechanisms. This results in a greater capacity to absorb information and an enhanced ability to migrate the new information from short-term to long-term memory. This is not surprising considering the fact that our brains contain the largest area of uncommitted cortex of any species–giving humans an ultra-flexible capacity for learning (*Brain Facts and Figures*, 2014).

(Jensen, 2008) epitomizes the underlying constructs in contemporary neuro-science, which inform our understanding of cognition in his work entitled "Brain-Based Learning: The New Paradigm of Teaching." Jensen illustrates the framework of Brain-Based Learning through the acronym 'ESP' whereby this popular 3-alphabet 'cliché' is representational of what is required to support the fundamental application of this process. As a construct—'E' = the active ENGAGEMENT of 'S' = purposeful STRATEGIES based on 'P' = PRINCIPLES derived from neuroscience.

This point is underscored by renowned physician and neuroscientist-turned educator Judy Willis in her work entitled "Brain-Based Teaching Strategies for Improving Students' Memory, Learning, and Test-Taking Success" (Willis, 2007). She highlights the emerging correlation between neuroscience and classroom instruction, noting that *"Now, educators can find evidence-based neuroimaging and brain-mapping studies to determine the most effective ways to teach, as advances in technology enable people to view the working brain as it learns."* (Willis, 2012) similarly contends, *". . . neuroscience research implications for teaching are also an invaluable classroom asset, it is time for instruction in the neuroscience of learning to be included as well in professional teacher education."*

More incredibly, some very basic facts about the brain reveal an astonishing organ, which consumes about 20% of the body's energy and constitutes a critical portion of the central nervous system. Comprised of nerve cells connected by nearly 1 million miles of nerve fibers, our brains use about 1/5 of the body's oxygen. The brain gets about 8 gallons of blood each hour (supplying nutrients like glucose, protein, trace elements, and oxygen) and requires 8-12 glasses of water a day to function at its best (*Brain Facts and Figures*, 2014).

As educators, teachers, and trainers, the ultimate goal of what we do is not too far removed from the results achieved by the inner workings of the brain. That is to coach, share, teach, and expose learners of all ages to information in a way that is long lasting and meaningful. Consider the voice of (Willis, 2006, Chapter 1) as she cogently states in "Research-Based Strategies to Ignite Student Learning." *"Learning promotes learning. Engaging in the process of learning actually increases one's capacity to learn."* With repetition of activities or content absorption, the brain's neural mechanism is strengthened and 'imprinting' of information or performance skills occurs.

The power of the brain lies in the degree of stimulation and nurturance it receives. The extent to which we feed it what it needs on a consistent basis can unleash an almost limitless capacity. The synergies derived generate more levels of creativity and make space for storage of more information. Such is the case because modern science has proven that people are unable to learn or absorb information when the brain is turned off.

Imagine the following scenario:

> Begin typing information on your computer and press the *"Enter"* key without checking to see if the machine has been turned on. Obviously, the computer will not work if it is not powered on. Similarly, just because we (humans) function on 'automatic pilot' for our most mundane actions, does not mean the computer (in this case our brain) is ready to work. The computer must be turned on to work. The same applies to our learners. One of our main responsibilities as educators and facilitators relative to our learners is to help ensure that the BRAIN is turned on.

The following chapters in this book contain dramatic engagers, the intrinsic components of which help to crystallize vital elements within the brain that are essential for learning and comprehension at meaningful and memorable levels. The reader will encounter multiple layers of informative content in Chapter Two. However, it is important initially to examine the six principles to creatively teach the whole brain. These principle—*movement, socialization emotional, meaning, safety, and enrichment* feed this organism.

Movement

When oxygen and glucose travel to the brain, this human organism functions at an increased rate. Physical movement plays a strong role in assuring that this process takes place and is an effective way of distracting the brain from daily stressors and negative thoughts. Exercise can generate a more relaxed state by producing endorphins—"the feel good neurotransmitter"—and ultimately stimulating the inherent desire for 'more of the same'. In addition, research offers further insights into the importance of motor development in brain functioning. Motor skills contribute substantially to an essential platform utilized by the brain in its sequencing of patterns needed for academic concepts.

In this connection, it is important to inform your learners of the strong correlation between movement and brain cognition. We found that sharing at least one objective and anticipated benefit of dramatic engagers to be a motivating factor for the learners. Informative communication can evoke a solid buy-in and commitment to the learning activities (Rogers, 2003). For instance, we discovered statements, such as, *"The more you move, the better your chances of nurturing the brain* and *the better your chances are for taking in new information"* to be helpful in our practice.

There are many opportunities throughout the dramatic engagers that involve kinesthetic 'hands-on' exercises, exertion, and movement. Most important, the physicality derived from utilizing these dramatic engagers will fuel the brain via the sensory of balance, coordination, spatial awareness, and visual literacy.

Socialization

Socialization acts as a major highway to brain engagement. The literature informs us that the brain functions at a higher rate when it is connected with other brains—creating a synergistic effect. Goleman notes, "our social interactions operate as modulators, something like interpersonal thermostats that continually reset key aspects of our brain function as they orchestrate our emotions (p. 6). In other words, creating healthy social interactions in the learning space increase the brain's capacity to develop and activate the neural bridge connection. For an extended period of time, neuroscience did not establish a direct correlation between socialization in the classroom and the brain's ability to change and grow. More recently, however, an expanding body of research findings offers definitive evidence that social intelligence is quite stimulating to the brains' ability to store more new information. Bolstering an awareness of this paradigm shift regarding socialization and cognition is fundamental—in fact critical—to education reform efforts across the country. It is imperative that our educators consider the benefits of constructive social and behavioral interactions during instruction periods.

Socialization inherently demands engagement and this construct coincides with the work of Gardner's multiple intelligences (2000). We now know how prominent it is to have positive social interactions during the learning process, specifically because it impacts and affects our cognitive development. Importantly, Jensen (2005) posits, "Data from multiple sources (social and behavioral studies using both physical data and functional neuroimaging) indicate that the development and influence of the social cognitive brain is not limited to just one area (p. 95). Another salient finding from contemporary research on learning, cognition and the brain is that embracing the natural organic connections between socialization and learning also builds relevancy for participants.

Emotional

Emotional context serves as the nexus for many of the creative strategies found in the book's succeeding chapters. Emotions provide a strong conduit for stimuli that help the brain learn. According to Jensen (2008), emotions are key when it comes to the brain in storing and its retrieval of information, particularly in shaping meaning to incoming data. Specifically, positive emotions stimulate the brain for learning and provide an organic method of garnering the brain's attention. Similar to an electrical switch plate, emotion charges the brain and serves to maximize how information travels throughout the organism. On the other hand, negative emotions typically drive the brain into a survival mode causing the brain's dendrites to come to a halt (Goleman, 1995). This is neither healthy nor productive for the brain.

Once positive energy and an aura of happy feelings and thoughts are present, the brain pays attention in a way that is beneficial to our learners. The process that arises from positivity is critical because it enables learners to absorb information as well as translate it into meaning. Therefore, this scenario enhances the opportunities for learners to become reflective thinkers, creative thinkers, critical thinkers, and problem solvers (Smilkstein, 2011).

Second, brain-based research informs us that the actual processing of new information creates an optimal environment within the brain for the transfer of new thoughts, ideas, and facts from short-term to long-term memory. Providing your learners with tools that aid them in storing new information in long-term memory results in an enhanced potential for absorption and recall. Positive emotions, prompted either internal or external in origin, help the brain release chemicals that promote intrinsic motivation—rendering the brain more adept at learning and retaining information.

Smilkstein (2011) recommends that educators consider the emotions of their students by establishing a supportive and respectful environment in the classroom. Highlighting the biochemical impact of emotions on learning, thinking, and remembering capacities within the brain, Jensen (2005) suggests that music, art, and group projects are beneficial and enriching because the literature reveals their positive effect on brain functioning.

Meaning

Meaning is more significant to the brain than information. Although the brain can take in information and process it, without the contextual meaning it will have a major effect on how the information is stored and how it maybe retrieved. It is important that we create a learning space that is meaningful. Instruction that is meaningful captures learners' attention. Gaining the attention of the learners' brain is one of the most critical functions of the dramatic engagers.

The brain's mechanisms are quite active so it is essential that we garner meaningful attention of this vital human organism so that we can help direct and enhance its natural pathways. You will become familiar with certain creative strategies over time through repetitive application of our dramatic engagers. In addition, the ease at which you are able to channel your learners' focus in the desired directions will amaze you!

Goleman (1995) eludes to several factors relating to emotional and brain distraction. In his discussion about getting the brain to pay attention and subsequent focus, his emphasis is not so much on countering the outside noises around us, rather the emphasis is placed on the disposition of our inner voices, which oftentimes arise from our emotions, particularly fear and anxiety. Quieting the brain so that new information can be stored is one of the most difficult things to accomplish. However, even more important, the brain must be rendered sufficiently attentive to move in a direction that is most productive for data retrieval to occur.

In discussing the work of Desimonde and Baldauf, Lightman (2014) asserts that what we perceive as "paying attention" to something originates at the cellular level in the synchronized firing of a group of neurons, the rhythmic electrical activity of which rises above the background chatter of the vast neuronal crowd. You will find that many of the creative strategies concentrate on warming up the brain, tension reduction, and releasing stressors, all of which are competing to signal the brain's attention. Once the brain becomes 'present' in the learning environment with the attention where it needs to be, the challenge for the instructor becomes maintaining its focus.

Safety

The brain instinctively wants be safe in its learning environment. According to Jenson (2008), the brain goes into a fight or flight effect if it feels threatened or in danger. Unfortunately, participants may consider learning environments as threatening by either competition, bullying, fear, and/or feelings of inferiority, lack of validation, as well as other external factors that prevent the brain from learning. The brain needs to feel safe in its learning environment, and the teacher/trainer can create a safe environment by providing opportunities for participants to build relationships with dramatic engagers.

Teachers/trainers must combat teats and potential in the room so that brain does not start to feed off of stress and tension. Behavior modification and classroom management play such a key role in the learning environment.

In chapter two, we provide a section that offers strategies that create a safe space for learning to take place. By lowering the stress and de-escalating tension the working space will in turn lower the chances for impaired learning and the depletion of brain cells. The brain just does not function or process information well when it does not sense safety.

Enrichment

Enrichment is the pathway to the brain that grows new connections for learners of all ages. More importantly, enrichment is known best for developing cognitive skills at the cellular level there is a stark distinction between an impoverished neuron as oppose to an enriched neuron. Neuroscientists' studies have demonstrated that "a student, when properly stimulated, can improve their intellectual quotient by as much as twenty points in a proper learning environment" (Jensen, 1998). Utilization of music before, during, or as a transitional entry-exit vehicle for the varied teaching strategies is a strong and exemplary tool that sets the stage for enrichment and stimuli to exist within the learning space.

The brain's stimuli readily emanate from sight. Imagine the magnitude of the brain's capacity to receive and process stimuli if we are able to activate and increase other senses like touch, smell, hearing, and taste. Our selected engagers allow you to activate and establish an enrichment environment where at least three different senses can inhabit simultaneously. Many of the instructional strategies are multi-sensorial in nature, which directly supports the brain, and (Jensen, 2008) stimulates creativity, thinking, and sensitivity.

Enrichment extends the door of opportunity for the brain to have stimuli that enables it to function fully at high capacity. Stimuli can affect the brain in ways that are both striking and nuanced. Not realizing this, teachers and trainers sometimes undermine their own power with their presentation, style, and non-verbal communication. For example, non-verbal cues, such as proxemics, kinesics, prosody, and immediacy all stimulate the brain. It is incumbent upon us to become more mindful of subtle non-verbal and verbal cues so that we can navigate within our environments from an enriched and nurturing stance—thereby making our jobs much easier.

Although we understand the significance of harnessing as many of the five senses as possible, something as subtle as eye contact, touching, smiling, and nodding can convey positive reinforcement to learners. In this same vein, however, we must also edit ourselves and be mindful of giving off negative non-verbal cues, such as pointing, hands on hip, frowning, stern look, and arms-crossed movements (Smilkstein, 2011).

As you review the material in this book and start to use the dramatic engagers, you will discover natural moments when you generate positive enrichment and stimuli for the brain simply by how you process the experiences at hand. In other words, if you review some of the processing strategies and questions in Chapter One, you may take on different roles and find your own tone. However, we encourage teachers and trainers to consider the following process roles to assume when initiating the dramatic engagers. Here are some suggestions when delivering opened-ended and closed-ended questions that can help stimulate the brain in a direct and warm manner. Review and consider what we have found to be the top 10 process roles:

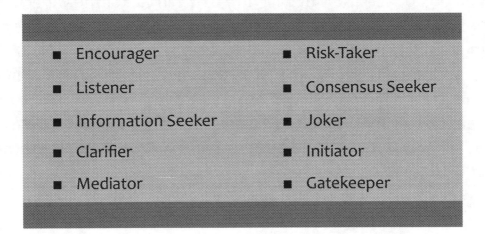

- Encourager
- Listener
- Information Seeker
- Clarifier
- Mediator
- Risk-Taker
- Consensus Seeker
- Joker
- Initiator
- Gatekeeper

Recognizing the enormous advantages of embracing these theoretical principles in a learning environment is crucial to understanding that the brain has a fundamental right to be properly turned on, warmed-up, and prepared to learn. Therefore, it is contextually important that we consider an assertive style of teaching that is purposeful, relevant, and respects cultural differences. Such an approach to teaching (arguably a best practice) increases our learners' chances to become 'winners of knowledge.'

In an unfortunate trend, however, contemporary curricula frequently over-emphasizes factual recall at the expense of emotional and character development. Increasingly, today's learning environments, regardless of the participant's age (youth or adult) or scenario (face-to-face classroom or E-learning formats), do not pay sufficient attention to ensuring that the brain has been properly powered (turned) on. In such instances, learners and educators often derive an opposite effect from the positive gains described above, therefore, finding themselves in an untenable, no-win situation.

Two leading practitioners in the vanguard of introducing creative dramatics to classroom settings, (Heathcote & Bolton, 1995), suggest that drama encompasses man's ability to identify with himself/herself <u>and</u> the intended learning objectives. It matters not whether you are in the theater or nestled in your own living room. If you are dramatizing, you are inevitably putting yourself in somebody else's shoes—realizing new perspectives, insights, and cognitive gains (Wagner, 1976).

ACTIVE AND COLLABORATIVE LEARNING

Why active learning and what does it look like? Whenever experiences stimulate *mental activity that lead to meaningful learning (cognition),* this is *active learning.* Mentally active learning of ideas and skills can occur while engaged in a variety of thought-stimulating activities (Rusbult, 2014). For instance, *direct learning* takes place when didactic methods are used formally to impart information. Direct learning can be a derivative of content absorption from educational webinars, Internet forums, or other multimedia presentation formats. Similar to direct learning but more experiential in approach is learning by discovery. Examples include empirical discovery from conducting an experiment, creative design, and problem-solving projects.

Many thought-stimulating activities can result in *active learning.* Productive *mental activity* can occur — with or without *physical activity* in which you "do" something — during a wide variety of mentally active experiences. Active and collaborative learning is commonly illustrated when groups of students work together to search for understanding, meaning, or solutions or to create an artifact or product of their learning (Smith & MacGregor, 1992). Collaborative learning is heavily rooted in Vygotsky's views that an inherent social nature of learning exists. His premise is highlighted by his theory of zone of proximal development (Lee & Smagorinsky, 2000). Further, collaborative learning redefines the traditional student-teacher relationship in the classroom, which almost paradoxically results in controversy over whether this paradigm is more beneficial than harmful. Collaborative learning activities can include collaborative writing, group projects, joint problem solving, debates, study teams, and other activities.

The literature informs us that students are apt to learn more when they are actively involved in their education and have opportunities to think about and apply what they are learning in different settings. Through collaborating with others to solve problems or mastering challenging content, students develop valuable skills that prepare them to cope with various situations and problems typically encountered in their workplace, communities, and personal lives.

Goal-directed instruction can be a motivational experience when students become stakeholders in their academic process by virtue of the relevancy of the curriculum to their daily lives and their concurrence with learning goals and objectives (Rusbult, 2002). When worthy goals are highly valued by students, the school experience is transformed from a shallow game (of doing what the teacher wants, with the short-term goal of avoiding trouble) into an exciting quest for knowledge in which the ultimate goal is a better life. When teachers and students share the same goals, education becomes a teamwork effort with an "us" feeling.

When students are highly motivated to learn, simply calling attention to a learning opportunity is sufficient. Instead of doing only what is required to complete schoolwork tasks, students will invest extra mental effort with the intention of pursuing their own goals for learning. Why? Because they are motivated by a forward-looking expectation that what they are learning will be personally useful in the future, and that it will improve their lives. They will wisely ask, "What can I learn now that will help me in the future?"

In relation to providing active and collaborative strategies in the classroom, research by (Kuh, 2001) identified student-teacher interaction as a distinct learning process for activities that reflect and integrate learning activities with students. (Kuh, 2013) further contends that collaborative assignments and projects are high-impact activities for student engagement—recommending these methods as a catalyst for instructors in collaborating and coordinating activities with students.

Active Collaborative entails the very notion that learners learn regarding different levels of intelligence (Gardner, 2000). Infusing creativity is necessary because it can attract and stimulate young and adult learners by engaging key influences on the learner. (Wenger, 1998) asserts that when we are with a community of practice, we learn certain ways of engaging in action with other people. Therefore, if we are going to motivate the educator/trainer to teach/coach and the student/participant to learn, we need to understand the people in the classroom and to look at it as a community in need of engagement in order to act in the teaching and learning processes. This book addresses not only the need for such a model but also the relevance of knowing that it can potentially impact an entire community in a transformative and humanizing way of teaching and learning.

UNDERSTANDING CREATIVE DRAMATICS

One of the difficulties in understanding and using creative dramatics is providing a clear definition of the term itself. The following terms have been used interchangeably: *developmental drama* (Cook, 1917), *creative dramatics* (Ward, 1930), *educational drama* (Way, 1967), *mantle of the expert* (Heathcote & Bolton, 1995) *informal drama* (Wagner, 1991), and *process drama* (O'Neill, 1995). These terms can be confusing at times, especially when one is seeking to understand the roots and context of drama integrated into a curriculum.

During the 1920s and 1930s in the United States, Winifred Ward (1957) is noted as the founder of creative drama, the central focus of which was to provide participants with the ability to unlock their personal creativity. Ward defines creative dramatics as "an inclusive expression designating all forms of improvised drama, dramatic play, story dramatization, impromptu work in pantomime, shadow, and puppet plays and all other extemporaneous drama" (Ward, 1957). Ward was known for working with the story dramatization technique with students and teachers in the elementary curriculum. Her special ways of devising, implementing, and rehearsing were generated by the story dramatization, but this technique dominated thinking in educational drama for the next 30 years.

McClasin (1990) also offers the definition adopted by the Children's Theatre Association of America: "Creative drama is an improvisational, non-exhibition, process-centered form of drama in which the participants are guided by a leader to imagine, enact, and reflect upon the human experience. Although creative drama has been thought of in relation to children and young people, the process is appropriate to all ages" (McClasin, 1990). Creative dramatics uses students' imaginations and willingness to act or pretend as a means of reinforcing academic, emotional, and interpersonal objectives (Bolton, 1979). Most important, educational drama and various other art forms help students to build solid connections with other academic areas and with the integration of the learning process (Wagner, 1976). Drama in and of itself (Johnson, 1998) promotes cross-cultural, interdisciplinary learning and interactive, inquiry-centered instruction, all of which help foster intellectual curiosity, self-discipline, and perseverance.

Creative drama differs from theater performed as scripted dialogue on a set in front of an audience. Instead, drama-in-education often involves an entire class in improvised roles within an imagined context or frame (Heathcote & Bolton, 1995). As a result, these dramas do not sharply distinguish between the actor and the audience: the learner is both participant and observer, playing roles while interacting with others in roles. The drama is facilitated by the classroom teacher who builds on the actions and reactions of students-in-roles to change, or reframe, the imagined context to create an episodic sequence of dramatic action (Levy, 1987).

Koziol & Richards (1996) provide a different perspective in describing what is meant by *Informal Drama*, a term that can be interchangeable with creative drama. "Informal Drama is often called play or improvisation at the elementary level and improvisation or role-play at the secondary level" in countries, such as Britain, Australia, and New Zealand. Some of the types of informal drama activities offered by Koziol & Richards (1996) include imagination exercises, movement exercises, sensory exercises, verbal exercises, pantomime, storytelling, choral reading/reader's theater, dramatization, improvisation, and role-play.

On the other hand, Rijnbout (1995) suggests that creative drama falls under the umbrella of educational drama. He further recommends that as users of educational drama, we recognize that although different age ranges may respond to different techniques, creative dramatics offers warm-ups both physically and emotionally and restores the element of "make believe" in the classroom.

Bolton's concept of educational drama and creative drama differs in that drama practitioners endeavor to help secure an emotional engagement of the student that underlies the desired learning area, which is not to say that the student's involvement with the activity (the form) should be gained at the expense of the meaning—the content. The drama should function on three main levels of meaning for the participants. Bolton (1979) describes it best as "the contextual, the universal, and the personal." Bolton's discussion of creative dramatics in an education has to project a summation of the whole experience, not only because it focuses on the feelings of the participants, but also because creative dramatics can offer a visual image that remains in one's memory, carrying contested, universal, and personal meanings simultaneously.

The listing below defines key terminology that refer to some of our favorite creative dramatic strategies and applications:

KEY TERMS

MOVEMENT RHYTHM	• Participants can use movement and body language as forms of self-expression. Often it is easier for a student to convey a feeling or idea through actions rather than words. The goal of the teacher is to teach children about the drama inherent in movement (Wagner, 1976).
HOT-SEATING	• In order to discover details about a character, the group interviews individual participants who remain "in role." Inquiries may be made in a formal question-and-answer session format or improvisations may be "frozen" in time and role-players "released" to answer questions put forth by the educator/facilitator (Rijnbout, 1995).
TABLEAU	• A frozen picture (photo, painting, cartoon, sculpture) can serve to crystallize an idea or communicate a concrete image. These images may be sculpted into another image, brought to life, or captioned. A prime example is a newspaper photo accompanied by a headline (Rijnbout, 1995).

SHOULDER TOUCH	• Shoulder Touch is an extension of Tableau/Still Image in which students select four parts from a Shoulder Touch. The student holding the 'frozen' position is tapped on the shoulder by the teacher as a signal for the student to express the thoughts of the character or prop she/he is portraying (Rijnbout, 1995).
SNAPSHOTS	• In Snapshots, a story or incident is selected and a frozen scene is created for each part. Typically, the teacher has students choose significant or controversial moments from a story to further illustrate these moments (Rijnbout, 1995).
FREEZE FRAMES	• Freeze Frames are a series of tableaux or still images, which type a sequence of events in a story (Rijnbout, 1995).
MURAL OR FRIEZE	• Mural or Frieze is also a series of still images; however, in this type of Tableau, the images are shown simultaneously (Rijnbout, 1995).
ROLE-ON-THE-WALL	• An image of a character is drawn on the board and students are asked to fill in the diagram by brainstorming the strengths, weaknesses, characteristics, appearances, identifying hopes and fears, and listing the many roles the selected character may have to play in society (Basom, 2006).
LEADER-IN-ROLE	• An individual who interacts with the participants (audience members) takes on a role that might control the action, excite interest, invite involvement, provoke tension, challenge thinking, create choices and ambiguities, or further develop the narrative (Rijnbout, 1995).
PANTOMIME	• Pantomime is the start of movement/hip-hop dance, strategically used to define truth. This technique focuses on the meaning revealed by the physical gestures and movements of a character rather than by vocal communication (Rijnbout, 1995).

ROLE-PLAYING	• This involves the spontaneous enacting of scenes, experiences, ideas, responses, and interpretations based on roles that are reasonably defined through previous discussion or text; in responding to issues or problem situations, children make choices based on their understanding of the characters (Koziol & Richards, 1996). The entire group is given specific roles, designed by the leader, in order to explore the situation of the drama. These roles can be defined by occupation (family counselors), relationship (members of a family in crisis), location (inhabitants of a small town), or attitude (political protesters). The group can assume the same roles or a combination of roles, depending on the needs of the particular workshop (Basom, 2006).
IMPROVISATION	• Improvisation is similar to pantomime, but the participants use dialogue. It involves a brief, unrehearsed situation or scene from a story in which the characters speak spontaneously. Impromptu speaking and acting can stem from situations, objects, sounds characters, ideas, problems, and unfinished stories. Puppetry and role-playing are two types of improvisation (Rijnbout, 1995).

THE POWER OF CREATIVITY

Throughout this book, we have stressed that cognition is best achieved when the brain mechanism is viewed as the central hub of the activity. Recognizing that instruction and learning are reciprocal processes and the engagement of the learner is of critical importance represents the crux of our message. As educators, researchers, and practitioners of creative dramatics and related modalities, creativity is a correlate element in achieving viable learner outcomes.

(Franken, 1994) defines 'creativity' as the tendency to generate or recognize ideas, alternatives, or possibilities that can be useful in solving problems, communicating with others, and entertaining others and ourselves. Creativity is a multilayered concept and viewed from various perspectives. Creativity involves cognitive, social, and environmental elements. the elements of creativity are interconnected: so much so that one element begins to feed off the other in an organic fashion. (Adams, 2005) writes in Sources of Innovation and Creativity: A Summary of the Research, "an explicit decision to be creative, along with a meta-cognitive awareness of the creative process" can do much to enhance "long-term creative results." The literature is replete with studies that illustrate the benefits of creativity as a distinct skill set and an attribute highly desired by employers across a range of industries. Career and technical education programs are devising programs that harness these capabilities in their students to enhance the global positioning options for America's workforce. Job applicants certainly need creative strategies. This is an undeniable fact, and so it is similarly important to research ways to advocate more teachers' use of creative techniques in the learning environment, especially for learners in need of non-traditional learning techniques. (Gardner, 2003) suggests the use of drama as a way to reach different types of intelligence because it connects to the audio, visual, and, especially, the aesthetic learning styles.

MAKING A CASE FOR SOCIAL AND EMOTIONAL DEVELOPMENT

Numerous learning theories have arisen from centuries of work by researchers, neuroscientists, theorists, and academicians. These learning theories, which have been cross-disciplinary and variable, include developmental, behavioral, cognitive, and social learning among the most prominent. From all indications, it seems apparent that 'learning' is an art form in itself, and one that continues to evolve over time. This is evident from the works of Piaget, Freud, Lev Vygostky, Bandura, and others. However, the most steadfast theme emanating from the constantly evolving field of brain-based research is that socio-emotional development is a critical element of brain functioning—serving as both an essential ingredient and stimulant for information processing.

We also know from brain research that affect (emotional presentation) and cognition (learning) work synergistically (together) — with emotion driving attention, learning, memory, and other mental activities (Zins, Weissberg, Wang, & Walberg, 2004, p. 24). In the world of academia, socio-emotional learning refers to the process of integrating thinking, feeling, and behavior to achieve important social tasks, meet personal and social needs, and develop the skills necessary to become a productive, contributing member of society (Zins et al., 2004, p. 27). The concept of socio-emotional development gained prominence from the works of (Goleman, 1995), (Goleman, 2006), and (Salovey & Mayer, 1990) specifically, their research on the significance of emotional intelligence.

A resource publication (University of Maine Center for Inclusion & Disability Studies, 2011) entitled, "Friends and Feelings: Social Emotional-Development in Young Children in Growing Ideas Toolkit" notes that "social" refers to how individuals interact with others. The word "emotional" refers to how individuals feel about themselves, others, and the world. Social and emotional development involves the ability to form close, secure relationships and to experience, regulate, and express emotions.

Social and emotional growth is an individualized process and affected by a variety of factors, such as a person's unique biological make-up and temperament, as well as their life experiences. Social and emotional learning are essential for the successful development of cognitive thinking and learning skills. In addition to understanding the emotional and social aspects of learning, research also confirms that learning is a natural process, inherent to all living organisms (Sternberg, 1997).

This section offers a discussion encouraging educators and trainers to broaden both their worldview and methodological perspective on instruction. First, ask yourself what methods do you already use in the classroom that might enhance the emotional and social development of your students? Second, what additional tools could be utilized in the classroom to expand the participants' social and emotional skill sets? This reflection has particular relevance to the manner in which educators share, provide, coach, and/or impart information to their learners.

Instructional methodologies are evolving overtime; however, educators are not embracing creative and variable techniques to the extent that is needed in contemporary academia. To a great extent, educators are not giving enough credence to differentiating instructional methods to accommodate differences in learning style—, which results in less than optimal comprehension rates (Kelly, 2014).

The strategies contained in this book are designed to aide you in communicating more effectively with students by infusing tools into the curricula and training manuals that help make learning an enjoyable experience. You will learn how to explore relationship issues that serve as a hindrance to learning. In fact, many such obstacles may even block both motivated and unmotivated learners from cognitive growth. Educators are now finding the emotional health of the students in their classroom to be more essential than ever. The creative strategies that you are exposed to throughout this book are not limited to the realm of socio-emotional development, however. Rather, these innovative methods and toolkits represent a formidable vehicle for enriching the learning climate.

When instructing and coaching both young and adult learners, the process of engagement and connection can be facilitated by focusing on attitudinal and behavioral factors surrounding the specific content area. Material is rendered more meaningful by this approach. The relevancy in focus generates a socio-emotional awareness around the specific content areas and helps build inquiry. Social elements in the learning process tap into the 'how' and 'why' people learn and communicate various acquired skill sets.

Emotional learning triggers one's innate ability to identify and express individual needs, thoughts, and feelings, along with negotiating conflicts and interpersonal relationships. Social and emotional learning places emphasis on critical-thinking skills, self- management skills, and refusal skills. These type of skill sets allow participants to gain a sense of self, as well as an understanding and empowerment that comes with taking responsibility for one's own socio-emotional health.

Over the years, we have established a style and perfected select drama-based strategies predicated upon brain-based learning theory, organizational development, relevant evidence-based practices—all undergirded by our own experiential knowledge and empirical observations. These elements are codified in a system of beliefs that enabled us to successfully design, implement, and engage students.

Leading theorists and practitioners have approached these strategies in different ways and this collage of theory, evidence-based and empirical driven practice serve as the basis for development of our conceptual framework. Garrison (2003) advocates that such techniques be used due to the climate of students in the 21st century. In addition, there are many theorists who emphasize that when creativity is used across the curriculum, not just in the language arts, it has proven to be an effective tool. Anderson (1992) also suggests that improvisational activities show students – in a demonstrable way – how various strategies can be utilized to organize their conversational demeanor. Such skills can empower participants to more effectively orchestrate the consequences of their social and academic experiences.

PROCESSING STRATEGIES FOR DRAMATIC ENGAGERS

After you conduct your first dramatic engager, what's next? Well, here is the moment to bring it all together or at least to invite the learners to assess and reflect on what they are learning and/or to further question what they have just experienced. Dramatic engagers explore a number of active collaborative strategies, which can be infused to curricula or training modules. Our listed dramatic engagers will enable you to explore character building, skill building, and set the stage for creative re-enactments that are some of the most engaging tools for connecting participants to content. The next step of moving into processing questions is salient in that it invites participants to examine the components of various constructs anywhere from language arts and historical periods to understanding the steps of CPR to de-escalating conflict in the workplace. You will notice that this book provides an intense listing of dealing with imagery work. Still images are used to engage and deepen the context as well as increase cognitive skills outside of the typical memorization regime. The result of the techniques and experiences will allow participants to personalize, reflect, and recall the projected information.

The processing of questions and transitions that support the critical learning areas is essential when implementing any of the dramatic engagers that you will embark on in the following questions. Last, it will specify the relevance of leading responsive cultural pedagogy, which is quite salient for most learners.

Creative strategies are implemented often without allowing the students to draw from their personal experience. Most practitioners focus disproportionately in avoiding interventions that penetrate the outer core of their participants' psyche so much on distancing what is happening when delving into different types of creative engagement from the youth's own sense of self in fear that it might strike up a conversation that touches on sensitive and controversial issues. It is our fundamental belief that we must provide safety nets when executing the dramatic engagers for the participants because we need to be responsible educators and to protect the emotional, symbolic, and physical well being of the child and the adult. However, once the dramatic engager and the sense of make-believe are over, it is also the responsibility of the educator/trainer to guide the learner to transfer the knowledge and then allow him/her to tap into her/his own unique way of thinking, believing, feeling, and listening to what truth is for him/her.

Perhaps as more of us in various subject areas start to pinpoint how and why certain pedagogical decisions are made and what influences certain choices, decisions will become more teacher- and student-driven. Heathcote would argue that creativity in the classroom is not complete until the right questions are asked (Wagner, 1976). Although there may not be right answers all the time, techniques should be in-place so that we can at least be open enough to engage the students through questions that help inform and deepen their understanding of the creative experience. Sometimes when a majority of diverse learners fills classes, the climate is so intense that there is insufficient time even to ask the questions the teacher or the students may wish to ask.

You may find yourself repeating your favorite five dramatic engagers all the time or perhaps you may do a number of them at different times for different audiences. Regardless of how many you do or where you do it, the next step is to process it! However, before any questions can be determined and answered, an understanding of the goals and functions of the drama first must be gained. Second, one must assess the extent of learning achieved through a dramatic experience as a direct result of questioning. The "open-ended question"—or what Dorothy Heathcote (Wagner, 1976) calls the "freeing" questions—promotes curiosity and frees the child to wonder. This is an extremely important point and aids in providing safety nets between the teacher/trainer and the trust factors between the teacher and the learners. Stephen Nachmanovitch (1990), author of *Free Play*, highlights the importance of freeing-up the suggested participants in order for them to receive information. (Nachmanovitch, 1990) concludes, "unblocking one's subconscious to a point where it can stimulate the conscious level of one's mind brings the discovering process to the surface."

Questions in drama have a very different purpose from the kind of traditional questioning that is often used by educators. Heathcote's suggested modes of questioning are simple and specific. There are questions that seek information or assess participant interest, including those that define the moment, those that stimulate research in books, or call for asking experts for information.

The second mode of questioning is often a difficult one in a learning environment with participants who have low self-esteem and/or poor attention spans because their raising their hands to give an answer where there is a specific right or wrong response to their thought becomes troubling at times. However, in the moment of engagement, there is so much information being given out that once the participants come out of the experience and have to return to their own thoughts and settle down, they seem to freeze for a moment and slowly begin to realize that they know the answer. This moment allows them to realize that they, too, can comprehend.

GUIDELINES FOR PROCESSING DRAMATIC ENGAGERS

Below you will find suggested questions that can assist during and after you have completed selected dramatic engagers. Remember that you are responsible for ensuring that you get your learning points out, so you must ask questions that support the objective and/or share specific information via a passage from a book, worksheets, chart, handout, PowerPoint, monkey survey, polling questions, instructional video, and/ or YouTube. Remember to process both their level of engagement and experience and how they processed information by asking a couple of simple questions.

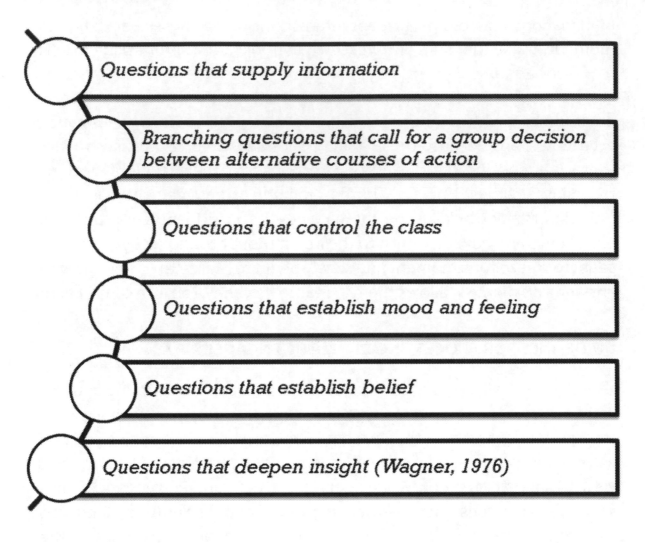

Questions that supply information

Branching questions that call for a group decision between alternative courses of action

Questions that control the class

Questions that establish mood and feeling

Questions that establish belief

Questions that deepen insight (Wagner, 1976)

40 SUGGESTED PROCESSING QUESTIONS
FOR DRAMATIC ENGAGERS

1   What worked well for you?

2   What surprised you the most when doing this dramatic engager?

3   What did you notice about those around you?

4   What skills are needed to be successful with this activity?

5   Did you notice any new skills that you needed to develop to become more fully engaged next time?

6   What was this dramatic engager like for you?

7   How did you feel about this process?

8   What did you notice was going on with the other people around you?

9   What skills did you use when doing the exercise?

10 What was difficult about this exercise?

11 What made this exercise easy to participant in?

12 Does this exercise remind you of anything as it relates to how we learn in life or how we interact with each other here?

13 What did you notice about your communications?

14 What did you observe about your non-verbal and verbal reactions?

15 Did you notice anything interesting about those around you aesthetically when it came to how they received and sent the different messages?

16 Did you learn anything new about yourself doing this exercise?

17 What did you find most challenging?

18 If you had the opportunity to do the exercise all over, what would you do differently?

19 Does anything about this exercise remind you of conflict?

20 How do you identify conflict?

21 What type of feelings and disposition happen when one is in a conflict?

22 How many people think that you handle conflict well?

23 What aspects of this exercise reminded you of how you or other people handle conflict?

24 What are the potential pitfalls when one does not confront a conflict?

25 What about this experience is different than placing your answers on a paper?

26 Are you comfortable with the way you have been studying the information?

27 Did you observe on the different questions the ideas or concepts that you need more help?

28 What did you notice about your choice of words as it related to this activity?

29 Did you notice anything differently about your writing style after doing this dramatic engager?

30 Did you change your words at any time and if so why?

31 Were most of your responses set or did you find yourself using the words or an image to help you think about what to say?

32 Did you notice any similarities to how you responded with others in the group?

33 Did any words or thoughts surprise you that were placed on the floor?

34 Did anyone share a word that might have changed how you thought about a specific topic/theme?

35 How does the meaning of one word or picture shape its value?

36 How do you feel right now?

37 Do you feel that others listened to you?

38 How did it feel to give your opinion by "putting yourself on the line"?

39 Were you surprised by the intensity of your feelings in the discussion?

40 Did you become more empathetic after stepping into another person's shoes?

Processing Strategies: Although we strongly suggest you process every exercise if time permits, you will notice that there are a few engaging activities that have the processing strategies embedded into the actual exercise. Therefore, there may not be a need to move into more processing. However, if there is specific feedback that you need to share, especially as it relates to how well they did or what you want to see more of next time or comment on any unexpected learning moments, behaviors, and attitudes, processing transition is a great time to infuse that into your working session.

Did you become more empathetic after stepping into another person's shoes? Have the participants reflect on how well they processed or did not remember specific facts or responses.

Share strategies that will increase a higher success rate next time. (Provide study habit information and open it up to those who did well and allow the participants to share their own tricks of the trade.)

Tell the participants, "Imagine if you were leading this activity. What questions or problems would you have tossed out to the group and if you can think of one, what would it have been"? Instead of asking them to just say it or to write it down, have them model it right there in the space. Ask questions that deal with how they processed the information. Ask questions that address the use of the five senses.

Illustrate the significance of taking the time to establish reciprocity, trust, and espris de corps among participants. In these scenarios, user-specific workshops cajole participants into an enhanced state of awareness, and productivity. In the highlighted strategies education, entertainment, and empowerment are interwoven to serve as a catalyst. Participants embark on a highly effective learning experience, which challenges them to maximize their potential, while simultaneously inspiring them to engage in introspection and critical analysis—thereby examining their academic and character deficits.

Chapter Two

Setting the Stage for Learning

The environment and culture of the classroom space can make or break a healthy learning continuum. The traditional learning space is set up with the teacher standing in the front and the participants SITTING in their chairs facing the board. The creative space has to be an environment where the participants can move around and form groups. However, the traditional participants are not used to this environment of teaching. Therefore, the teacher/trainer must engage them from the beginning and set the tone that this learning experience is going to be different. Of course, every participant is not going to be willing to change his/her traditional way of learning, so the teacher/trainer must create and set the right STAGE.

GENERAL TIPS FOR RESISTERS

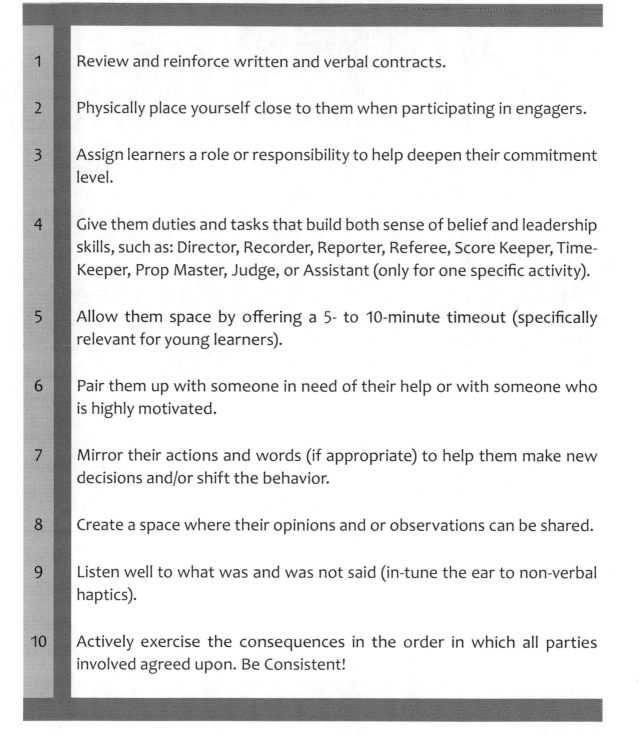

1   Review and reinforce written and verbal contracts.

2   Physically place yourself close to them when participating in engagers.

3   Assign learners a role or responsibility to help deepen their commitment level.

4   Give them duties and tasks that build both sense of belief and leadership skills, such as: Director, Recorder, Reporter, Referee, Score Keeper, Time-Keeper, Prop Master, Judge, or Assistant (only for one specific activity).

5   Allow them space by offering a 5- to 10-minute timeout (specifically relevant for young learners).

6   Pair them up with someone in need of their help or with someone who is highly motivated.

7   Mirror their actions and words (if appropriate) to help them make new decisions and/or shift the behavior.

8   Create a space where their opinions and or observations can be shared.

9   Listen well to what was and was not said (in-tune the ear to non-verbal haptics).

10   Actively exercise the consequences in the order in which all parties involved agreed upon. Be Consistent!

• LIVE CASE RESPONSES FROM RESISTERS •

1. • *I thought this was going to be hard and no one was going to do it*

2. • *I like the chance to see my peers have fun*

3. • *To watch my co-workers move like me when certain calls were placed on floor*

4. • *"We worked as a team, I didn't think that could happen in here"*

5. • *"We listened to each other and followed the directions"*

6. • *"We got to make things up on the spot"*

7. • *"We helped each other out when someone got stuck"*

8. • *"I didn't know he liked the same books as me"*

9. • *"This took me back some years I forgot how good it felt just to play"*

10. • *"I liked "all around the city" the best because everyone participated and we had fun, no fighting and stuff"*

11. • *"I like trying to do the different cartoon and TV characters and trying to beat the other team to the answer"*

12. • *"I can't pick a favorite all of the warm-ups were good, I mean you know we had fun, all just laughed and learned a lot and it was different you know"*

WARMING UP PARTICIPANTS

What we have found while implementing these dramatic engagers is that it is essential to take time to set up the classroom and establish a physical and mental space that is conducive to learning. Taking the time to 'Warm-Up' your learners is similar to setting the stage for actors to enter and begin a performance. This 'priming' influences the attitude and behaviors of learners. However, what is most critical is that this preliminary activity most immediately engages the brain.

The essential value of the warm-up process should not be underestimated. Take into consideration that many participants come into the learning space with bowed heads, saddened facial expressions, anxieties about academic achievement, and the burdens of peer pressure. In addition, let us not forget those individuals who appear un-kempt, have not eaten breakfast, or those who display little or no interest in learning at all. Conversely, you may encounter participants who enter the classroom with such zeal that they wake you up. Some come in with energetic smiles, singing, hugs, and jokes, hungry to learn standing or sitting with tools (e.g. PowerPoints), booklets, books, and pens in hand. Unfortunately, the latter contingent is fewer in number compared with other students who appear disenfranchised on a daily basis.

Educators have used warm-ups for years but for varied reasons and in different contexts. We advocate the use of warm-ups to help balance the classroom energy, to set the tone, and to establish our parameters for the learning process. Warm-ups have served as a lure for our main instructional activities—and prepared the young people's physical and mental well being. From empirical observation, documentation, and videography, we have captured key areas where the warm-ups settled the high-spirited students, calmed those who were in distress, energized the down-trotted spirits, and focused all of them to a space where the learning could begin. It is also important to note that while the warm-up exercises are taking place, cognition and skill-building elements are occurring simultaneously.

An automatic imbalance ensues in most classrooms within the first 10 minutes of each session. As leaders, instructors are left with the huge responsibility of teaching while attempting to discern the venue. For example, on one end of the room there may be absolute chaos, on the other end solemnity, and somewhere in the middle, there may be those who appear indifferent. As we amassed our body of work over the years, we meticulously documented and assessed the defining aspects of any pedagogy that garnered 100% learner participation. **WHY?** It was critical to know what strategies were viable. **WHAT DID WE LEARN?** We found that the 100% participation rates accrued from deployment of our dramatic engagers with the science behind the brain in mind.

As the leader of dramatic engagers, we have discovered this emergent theme, self-initiation. Through a number of participatory observations involving young and adult learners, coupled with intensive empirical assessments, we have found self-initiation significant for participants' success and equally crucial for educators because we start to deepen our metacognitive skills. This robust skill set is neglected often. Practitioners do not further develop the ability to activate and make room for metacognitive analysis and self-reflective practice to flourish.

It is fascinating to grasp how effective we allow ourselves to be when we are able to:

1) Engage in practice
2) Make spot-on assessments
3) Evaluate the results
4) Manage the process
5) Participate simultaneously

Brain warm-ups are definitely set-ups for a successful learning environment. In addition, the return on your investment once you allow yourself to practice any of our dramatic engagers is twofold. Although this book emphasizes the benefits for both young and adult learners, it is pertinent that we consider the benefits to the leader of these strategies. It harkens back to that huge question in Chapter One, "What's in it for you?" There are going to be times when you are burnout, under the weather, frustrated, overloaded, or simply overwrought with assignments and tasks. However, just by doing one of the 50 engagers you, too, will be stimulated in an uncanny yet meaningful way. As teacher, trainers, facilitators, educators, and whatever title we are endowed with, we too must continue to find ways to take care of our own psychological needs and motivate ourselves.

Our learners typically ask the anchor question posed in Chapter One, "What's in it for me?" However, Chapter Two sheds light on a different question—one that should be asked by the leaders and facilitators of the learning experience. Specifically: "What motivates our learners to learn?" This question is not new to academia but the responses have traditionally honed in on extrinsic motivational factors, such as incentives, money, extra points, more face-to-face time with a peer or co-worker/manager, certificates, and correlate variables associated with external learner motivators. With the advantage of additional brain research, we now know that a more formidable motivator for students can be found in intrinsic elements. Intrinsic rewards are considered more substantial and sustainable than short-term extrinsic factors.

Contemporary neuroscience has revealed the brain to be naturally curious and willing to seek out new experiences without any perceivable external reward. This natural curiosity breeds an internal motivation to learn. Nourishing the brain and providing a setting that is conducive to preparing the brain for learning is a more meaningful motivator than external rewards. By tapping into the curiosity of students with "hooks" or "discrepant events" at the beginning of a lesson, teachers are able to generate naturally curious and, therefore, motivated, students (…website teach the mind… 2014).

Classroom Management

Dramatic engagers help set a tone and are embedded with *managerial protocols,* perfect for the classroom and supports learners in a way that enable them to work to their fullest potential. It is imperative that we facilitate safe experiences so that all learners may find their entry and departure points and sufficiently transition into open and honest discourse. After introductory exercises and processing the experience, introduce your learners to creative classroom management techniques.

Throughout the years, we have noted that there are some creative managerial protocols that just work well in almost every setting regardless of the age range in your classroom. This section contains particularly good information for those who work in a face-to-face classroom environment. The top three management techniques appeared to work really well:

1) *Demanding Physical and Vocal control—"FREEZE"*
2) *Acquiring Visual and Cognitive Attention—"FOCUS"*
3) *Call and Response requiring verbal repetition awareness of information— "May I have Quiet on the Set?" "Yes, You May."*

Our personal research and empirical observation of these techniques clearly emphasized participants' receptivity to these creative techniques. It was apparent that participants, educators, and staff development facilitators equally embraced our methodologies. In addition, by reviewing the 'self-reflections' feedback from instructors, we gained a deeper insight into some of the rationale behind our effectiveness—even in the most resistant work environments (which ran the gamut of anywhere between adjudicated committed youth to mandatory managers and disgruntle staffers' professional development seminars).

Practical Application Tips

Gallien and Peterson (2005) assert that *call and response* reflects oneness, interdependence, participation, and attempts to bring together the speaker and the listener (p. 78). "May I have Quiet on the Set?" attracts participants because it allows them to be rhythmical and repetitive in the process, which works wonderfully when one is trying to foster a brain-based environment. Explain to the group that they will be working as a team for a number of sessions to explore the issues and to develop interpersonal skills, character, and enhanced communication abilities. This is a good time to introduce management techniques, such as "Freeze," "Focus," and "May I have Quiet on the Set?".

"Freeze" is a call only the teacher/trainer can use; and once stated, everyone must freeze. When you say, "Freeze. *There is to be no talking, walking, or blinking with eyes. The only thing you can do is breathe."* As you place and use these management strategies, it is critical that you model them while you are speaking. In other words, you too must freeze while communicating that message verbally. While introducing the freeze concept you may want to play around with its concept by saying, *"Only I can relax now but everyone else must continue to stay frozen. Let me test you guys out."* Then go around my frozen statuette participants, playing around with them, trying to get them to break their frozen positions and to break those serious faces. The only way you can get them out of the freeze mode is to say, "OK, now relax everyone."

"Focus" is another management technique—getting all class members to pay close attention to specific items, concepts, persons, or anything in drama that calls for students to concentrate. Actual documented responses from my students include, *"Do you all know what the word "Focus" means? It means to look at, to pay attention, or to be still."* After that, affirm all of their responses. Then, provide the description of Focus and say, *"Let's practice focusing, everyone. Everyone focus on Sheree, focus on the ceiling, focus on the window, the floor, oh no, I didn't say focus on the floor this time."* So here we were all able to put the technique right into practice.

"Call and Response," "May I have Quiet on the Set?" The participants respond with "Yes You May." This call/response technique works extremely well with active learners.

Another highly effective strategy is *"Head's Up!"* — especially in large learning environments. Here the leader calls out "Heads Up!" and participants respond by putting their hands on their heads and not speaking.

In perhaps what may seem counterintuitive to what you have read thus far in this book, we must also highlight the importance of allowing the creative process to evoke discomfort in your participants. It is interesting to watch how their vulnerability ultimately turns into security. Throughout our experiences, we know when to push a bit more and/or not to push at all. This comes from years of practice, self-reflection, and evaluation.

The Contract

After introducing management and participant protocols, now is a great time to have the class establish a contract together. The contract is a mutual agreement designed to create an atmosphere of trust, honesty, commitment, and safety. It is important that you invite participants to demonstrate their commitment to these norms by signing or initialing the contract where the norms have been outlined. Inform the participating community that the norms will be posted each time this group meets, which serves as a reminder of our commitment.

Explain to the participants that they are responsible for making sure that each new member of this community needs to know the norms and how they were established. Inform participants that they are expected to remind each other of the norms should anyone forget or violate them. Have a mini-discussion on the appropriate ways to remind one another.

Setting the Atmosphere

We encourage all educators, trainers, and facilitators to utilize fully the medium of sound, lyrics, and melody—and to not be afraid of playing music. Music is empowering by itself. In addition, if you find the appropriate music selection and infuse it alongside your learning objectives, you will not be at risk of it upstaging you or the learning process. If you wish to enhance what you already know to be working in your various instructional practices, and then finding that perfect instrumental piece (classical, jazz, or loud, unsynchronized sounds of rock and rap) can only unlock and magnify the information-processing experience.

This element of harmony deepens the quality of your educational instruction and is attractive and palatable to diverse learning styles. It is just as important for the leader to 'hear' a harmonious spirit when interacting with the drama techniques as it is for the students. I came to understand this type of sound because it was filled with positive energy and the tones of children—yielding bright affect and joyous sounds. Sometimes the sound was tempered by the peacefulness of other students. Although less verbal, their mannerisms and behaviors contributed to the harmonization—and even in their silence, their harmony rang out.

Making musical choices for classes should be predicated upon knowledge about your population—particularly regarding culture and ethnicity. For example, music in the classroom supported the learning process for some students. Moreover, the presence of music helped change the atmosphere and led to and enhanced understanding of socio-emotional aspects of the drama education modality for all learners. If you find yourself in a situation where the music and drama reach a crescendo or descend into a cacophony of sounds, then we would encourage you to take the risks allowing the unstructured moment to live and breathe in 'real time.' What does that really mean? To simply let it happen. What is most empowering as the leader is that you have the chance to act like that's exactly what you wanted to see happen and enjoy the moment. Never panic! Never let them see you sweat!

After you have gone along with whatever the upstaged moment might present, you will find it much easier for the learners to receive any information that you want to deliver. This is because you did not reject honoring their raw and 'in-the-moment' reactions. However, by opting to celebrate the opportunity of having it appear as though you meant it to happen, this still keeps you in charge of session, yet tears down those unforeseen barriers among your participants.

Using the Creative and Authentic Voice

An engaging educator typically has an engaging voice. A significant number of learners respond quite well to an emotive voice, which is energetic, well projected, and tends to be direct. Those leading these educational exercises that typically have soft and/or monotonous sounds find their voices being ignored or misunderstood. This is especially the case with more active learners. We do not have time to lose our voice—literally or figuratively. Every second matters and every learner's (youth or adult) attention span is unique. Therefore, we recommended that you find the power in your voice and own those teachable moments by developing your best creative voice.

In other words, the strategy refining the vocal tone is a critical part of setting the stage for creativity to exist with maximum quality. The voice tone, objective, and physical attributes should be present— all of this enables participants to buy into the process, as students are more in tune to your voice inflections. The use of these simple criteria can reveal— a sense of integrity and trust are manifested in a way that learners coax the leader to go further and the drama is enriched.

The next phase of developing your creative voice is to realize that it must be filled with inflections. The voice's targeted tone, along with the inflections, should tell a story with or without words. No, we do not mean to hold tones and to turn it into a song. However, the voice must be elevated and placed where you know the participants recognize that this is a unique and different sound that beacons attention. By identifying your best voice, you provide a greater chance to gain the brain's attention. The more stimuli and attention, the greater the impact will be on the brain receiving, processing, and retaining new information.

As the leaders of dramatic engagers, we have discovered the emergent theme of self-initiation, which is not significant just for the participants' success but for us as educators and trainers because we start to deepen our metacognitive skills. It is fascinating how effective we allow ourselves to be when we can: 1. Engage in practice, 2. Make spot-on assessments, 3. Evaluate the results, 4. Manage the process, and 5. Participate simultaneously. This robust skill set is what we often neglect or do not allow to develop further. The ability to activate and make room for metacognitive analysis and self-reflective practice to exist is essential to our growth and expansion.

Brain warm-ups are definitely set-ups for a successful teaching and learning environment and the return on your investment once you allow yourself to practice any of the dramatic engagers is twofold. Although this book emphasizes the benefits for both young and adult learners, it is pertinent that we consider the benefits for the leader of these strategies. It goes back to that huge question in Chapter One, "What's in it for you?" There are going to be times when you experience burnout, are under the weather, frustrated, overloaded, or simply run out of assignments and tasks. However, by doing 1 of the 50 engagers, you too will be stimulated in an uncanny yet meaningful way. As teachers, trainers, facilitators, educators, or whatever title we are endowed with, we too must continue to find ways to take care of our own psychological needs and motivate ourselves

We must create a space for students to learn, and when they are engaged, you can teach them the world. It is so much easier for me to teach about historical concepts and dates. When students are motivated and focused on content, they then know that the information matters to their everyday life. I would rather spend 5-6 minutes before the start of going into the main content area of the any session rather than raising my voice, convincing, and coaxing the learners for the full 45 minutes.

The famous philosopher Horace Mann was once quoted as saying . . . "A teacher who is attempting to teach without inspiring the pupil with a desire to learn is hammering on cold iron." In this connection, I could not agree more. Are active collaborative strategies worth it? Absolutely! However, even more so—the exercise strategies outlined in the following chapters are SIMPLY ENGAGING!

Chapter Three

Engagers That Prepare the Brain for Learning

The first series of creative exercises affords educators and leaders with the opportunity to stimulate and 'warm-up' the brain in preparation for its vital information-processing function. The diverse and user-friendly activities presented in this initial section allow for multi-sensorial-level stimulation of the brain. Second, these scenarios and instructive 'vignettes' help focus the brain, and at the same time, strengthen this complex organism's capacity for absorption and application of variable learning styles to process incoming information and stimuli.

Please take note of this major caveat. Never take for granted that the brain is always 'on' or perpetually 'functional' and ready to learn. These exercises represent a treasure trove of useful alternatives to assist you with increasing the chances of your learners tuning in and turning on their brain switch.

Sternberg (1997) in a special edition of American Psychologist emphasizes the fact that educators must be attune to their learners and devise lesson plans accordingly with the end-users' brain in mind. It is also important for teachers and parents to understand that maturation of the brain greatly influences learning readiness. Preparing the brain for learning is a significant instructional concept, and this cognizance helps to inform curriculum development for diverse audiences and learning styles. Moreover, this essential 'first step' in both teaching and learning frames the mindset of participants—serving as a bridge from a dormant state to active awareness that it's time to learn something new, review prior knowledge, and/or reflect on instructional or procedural facts. All of the strategies found in this chapter have the inherent ability to warm-up the brain, motivate learners, and increase learning capacities to enable critical information to move from the short-term memory to the long-term memory.

1

Countdown

BRAIN-BASED OBJECTIVES

To reduce threat and stress

To enrich the learning environment

To grab participants' attention

To give the brain a break

GROUP SIZE

Four or more

SPACE REQUIREMENTS

Classroom size

TIME

5 to 10 minutes

FUNCTIONS

(Energizer, Problem Solving, Social Skills, Focus Activity)

PROCEDURE

1. The teacher/trainer asks participants to stand in a circle, and then asks them to whole hands with their eyes closed with their heads facing the ground.

2. Once all of the participants' eyes are closed and their heads are down, the teacher/trainer tells participants that they must count down from 20 to 1 as a team with 2 or more team members saying a number at the same time.

3. If two or more team members say the same number, the team must start back all over each time at 20.

VARIATIONS

1. Have teams countdown to 10 if the group is larger.

2. Place participants in groups and have them compete to see who can countdown before the other team. However, if the participants are placed in a group ranging anywhere between 6 and 10, the countdown should be set at 20.

2

Crossover

BRAIN-BASED OBJECTIVES

To reduce threat and stress

To enrich the learning environment

To grab participants' attention

To integrate physical activity

GROUP SIZE

Four or more

SPACE REQUIREMENTS

Classroom size

TIME

5 to 10 minutes

FUNCTIONS

(Content Building, Social Skills, Focus Activity)

PROCEDURE

1. The teacher/trainer must divide the participants into two groups.

2. Ask one group to stand on one side and the other group to stand across the other group facing each other. We suggest that the two lines should be a good 4-feet apart from each other so that one group is parallel to the other. Both lines of participants should be facing one another.

3. Then say, "I will place a statement or question out on the floor and you respond to the answer by crossing over to the other side and joining the line on the other side of the room." Switching places from one side of the room to the other side is a non-verbal response to the different questions and statements.

4. Give your participants a third option other than making absolute yes and no or like and dislike responses. Say, "You can move to the middle of the two parallel lines, which may indicate you have a response or reaction but it isn't an absolute."

5. Be as creative as possible when preparing your questions and or statements for your learners.

VARIATIONS

1. Create questions that require participants to crossover about their worldviews, values, and beliefs system (here you stay away from factual information). For example, say, "Crossover if you think carrying a concealed weapon should be legal." or "Crossover if you think uniforms are better than wearing your own clothing."

2. Eliminate the physical structure of crossover. Instead, invite participants individually to answer the questions immediately. Then, ask subgroup members to discuss a topic that surprised or inspired them.

3

Earthquake

Suggested Prop List
- ☐ Director's Slate
- ☐ Ball
- ☐ Construction Paper
- ☐ Dry Eraser Boards
- ☐ Colorful Scarves
- ☐ Pens, Pencils, Markers
- ☐ Play Microphone
- ☒ Movable Chairs

BRAIN-BASED OBJECTIVES

To enrich the learning environment

To grab participants' attention

To integrate physical activity

To invite choices and self-direction

GROUP SIZE

Ten or more

SPACE REQUIREMENTS

Empty space to move around

TIME

15 to 25 minutes

FUNCTIONS

(Team Building, Energizer, Social Skills)

PROCEDURE

1. The teacher/trainer places two chairs side-by-side facing different directions around the room.

2. The teacher/trainer pairs the participants with someone who is close to their height and size, and asked to lock arms with their partner after sitting down beside one another.

3. The teacher/trainer gives each pair a number, and informs everyone that one of the pairs of chairs will act as the earthquake chair. The pair that is sitting in that area will still have a paired number that they will have for the remainder of the engager.

4. The teacher/trainer tells the participants that he/she will call out numbers, and if your number is called, you have to move to an empty paired chair set. If the teacher/trainer says "earthquake" all of the participants have to move to another chair.

5. The pairs must move to empty chairs without letting go of the arms of his/her partner. If a pair ends up in the earthquake chair or releases the arm of their partner, they receive a point against them.

VARIATIONS

1. Instead of chairs, you can have the participants stand up and move to a marked location on the floor.

2. Have participants in individual chairs without a partner. Instead of numbers, have them move if they agree with the statement from the teacher/trainer.

4

Fruit Bowl

Suggested Prop List
☐ Director's Slate
☐ Ball
☐ Construction Paper
☐ Dry Eraser Boards
☐ Colorful Scarves
☐ Pens, Pencils, Markers
☐ Play Microphone
☒ Movable Chairs

BRAIN-BASED OBJECTIVES

To enrich the learning environment

To stimulate the senses

To grab participants' attention

To integrate physical activity

GROUP SIZE

Six or more

SPACE REQUIREMENTS

A clear space where chairs can be in a circle

TIME

10 to 15 minutes

FUNCTIONS

(Energizer, Social Skills, Focus Activity)

PROCEDURE

1. The teacher/trainer places chairs in a circle and asks participants to sit down in the chairs. There must be enough chairs for all of the participants in the circle and the teacher/trainer places himself/herself standing in the middle of the circle.

2. Next, the teacher/trainer assigns each participant the name of one of three fruits (apple, orange, or pear), and the teacher/trainer assigns himself/herself a fruit as well.

3. The teacher/trainer calls out the name of a fruit and all the participants assigned to this category must switch seats. If he/she calls out, "Fruit Bowl," all of the participants regardless of their assigned fruit must move to an empty chair. The classmate who is standing in the center becomes the person who calls out one of the fruits or "fruit bowl."

VARIATIONS

1. Instead of chairs, you can have the participants stand up and move to a marked location on the floor (spotting the area with tape works well).

2. Have participants move if the person in the middle says something that is related to him/her. For example, the teacher/trainer can say, "Move if you like pizza." If the teacher/trainer wants everyone to move, they can say, "All Around the City."

5

Give Me Liberty

> **BRAIN-BASED OBJECTIVES**
>
> To enrich the learning environment
>
> To stimulate the senses
>
> To grab participants' attention
>
> To integrate physical activity

GROUP SIZE

Five or more

SPACE REQUIREMENTS

Classroom size

TIME

5 to 10 minutes

FUNCTIONS

(Energizer, Problem Solving, Social Skills, Critical Thinking Skills, Focus Activity)

PROCEDURE

1. The teacher/trainer asks participants to stand in a circle facing each other. The teacher/trainer places himself/herself in the middle of the

circle and finds three of the participants to explain the directions of the energizer.

2. The teacher/trainer lines up the three volunteers and models by pointing to the participant in the middle saying that if he/she points to you and says, "The Monument," the participant must stand up straight with his/her hands to his/her side and his/her head lifted high.

3. If the teacher/trainer points to you and says, "The Capital," the participant in the middle must use his/her arms to make a point of the dome and the two participants on each side of the participant must physically make round ends of the dome.

4. If the teacher/trainer points to a participant and says, "The White House," the participant in the middle must physically put his/her hands straight up and the participants on each side create columns. If the teacher/trainer points to a participant and says, "Give Me Liberty," the participant in the middle holds the flag, the participant on the right acts as if they are playing the drums, and the person on the left pretends to play the flute.

5. The goal for the participant is to create the images before the teacher/trainer counts to five. If any of the participants gets one of the physical positions wrong, the participant is eliminated from the engager.

VARIATIONS

1. Ask the participants to build other symbols instead of national monuments (these can be images that represent specific content areas).

2. Select two people in the circle who are not close to one another and do the exercise as described in the Procedure section. However, the big difference is that the other members inside of the circle must go support and lend help to the members who are outside of the circle while still maintaining the overall objective of the exercises. This is the higher-order format of this engager, which promotes team support and combats isolation.

6

Help or Hurt

BRAIN-BASED OBJECTIVES

To engage emotional learning

To find personal motivation

To cultivate meaning

To invite choices and self-direction

GROUP SIZE

Ten or more

SPACE REQUIREMENTS

Empty space to move around

TIME

10 to 15 minutes

FUNCTIONS

(Energizer, Social Skills, Focus Activity)

PROCEDURE

1. The teacher/trainer tells participants that they are to walk around the space and choose one of the other classmates to be their help and

another to be their hurt. The participants must choose two people without letting them know that they are chosen.

2. When the teacher/trainer says, "go," the participants walk around the space placing themselves behind their help as a shield and attempting to stay away from the classmate that they chose act as their hurt.

3. It is important to watch the passing of the group, as it may start slow and speed up or it may start fast and you can slow the movement down.

VARIATIONS

1. Have the participants use "bomb" and "shield" instead of "help" and "hurt" and process the significance of the metaphor as it relates to present-day life and/or a learning objective.

2. Have the participants choose two people who represent their help instead of one, but you can only identify one person to act as your help.

7

In Good Company

BRAIN-BASED OBJECTIVES

To enrich the learning environment

To stimulate the senses

To grab participants' attention

To integrate physical activity

GROUP SIZE

Six or more

SPACE REQUIREMENTS

Classroom size

TIME

10 to 15 min

FUNCTIONS

(Team Building, Energizer, Problem Solving, Social Skills, Critical Thinking Skills, Focus Activity)

PROCEDURE

1. The teacher/trainer asks participants to stand in a circle facing his/her classmates. The teacher/trainer places himself/herself in the middle of the circle explaining that the participants are to switch places with other classmates.

2. While the participants are switching places, the teacher/trainer is trying to get into one of the participants' space. Once the teacher/trainer grabs someone's space, a new participant is left in middle.

3. It is the responsibility of the participant who is in the middle to seek a new space once all parties in the circle start to move around.

VARIATIONS

1. Have participants use chairs instead of standing up. The participant who is left without a chair is stuck in the middle.

2. Follow all the steps in the procedure section. but it must be executed using only non-verbal communication. This variation will raise the stakes, heighten other senses, and encourage strategic planning to take place.

8

Zip-Zap-Zop

BRAIN-BASED OBJECTIVES

To reduce threat and stress

To stimulate the senses

To grab participants' attention

To give the brain a break

GROUP SIZE

Three or more

SPACE REQUIREMENTS

Classroom size

TIME

10 to 15 minutes

FUNCTIONS

(Team Building, Energizer, Problem Solving, Social Skills, Critical Thinking Skills, Focus Activity)

PROCEDURE

1. The teacher/trainer asks the participants to form a circle. Once everyone is standing up in the circle, he/she then asks everyone to speak the words ZIP, ZAP, ZOP.

2. The teacher/trainer explains that participants must point to one of the participants and say ZIP, the next person must say ZAP, and the other person must say ZOP.

3. After going through the consecutive order one time, you must repeat the process recurrently until someone speaks out of turn. In other words, you cannot say "Zip Zop" because that is out of sequence and it must move randomly around the circle in the specified order of ZIP, ZAP, ZOP.

VARIATIONS

1. Have the participants to add a "Bong" to the Zip, Zap, Zop, which acts as a reflecting mirror. The use of "Bong" is a clever way to pass, but the work is on the person who gets "Bong" because they are charged with remembering the message they originally sent out, which can only be Zip, Zap, Zop.

2. Instead of using Zip, Zap, Zop, you can create your own words and/or use it as a way to introduce a new language, concept, or period. For example, Thee, Thy, Thine can be used.

Chapter Four

Engagers That Develop Team Building

This second section of engagers contained in Chapter Three focuses substantially on the organization, definition and development of healthy productive teams. Here you will discover a noteworthy array of creative exercises, which can facilitate the delicate process of establishing an egalitarian and participatory atmosphere within the learning venue. Importantly, the suggested teambuilding engagers will assist in building a rapport with your learners as well as deepening the interaction among participants. These types of engagers allow the facilitator to create a 'zone of comfort and trust', which ultimately lures-in all participants in the room.

Rusbult (2002) discusses the motivational aspects of teamwork in education by stressing, "goal-directed teaching is easier if students are motivated by their own desires for goal-directed learning, and if there is agreement about goals." When worthy goals are highly valued by students, the learning experience is transformed from a shallow game (of doing what the teacher wants, with the short-term goal of avoiding trouble) into an exciting quest for knowledge in which the ultimate goal is a better life. When educators and either young or adult learners share the same goals, education becomes a team effort with an "us" feeling.

9
Add-on-Scene

Suggested Prop List
- ☐ Director's Slate
- ☐ Ball
- ☐ Construction Paper
- ☐ Dry Eraser Boards
- ☐ Colorful Scarves
- ☐ Pens, Pencils, Markers
- ☒ Play Microphone
- ☐ Other

BRAIN-BASED OBJECTIVES

To enrich the learning environment

To grab participants' attention

To integrate physical activity

To invite choices and self-direction

GROUP SIZE

Five or more

SPACE REQUIREMENTS

Classroom size

TIME

10 to 20 minutes

FUNCTIONS

(Team Building, Communication Skills, Social Skills, Content Building, Critical Thinking Skills, Focus Activity)

PROCEDURE

1. The teacher/trainer asks one participant to go up front and pantomime doing an activity. The activity could be something like working out in a gym or playing at the playground or baking a cake.

2. Once the other participants figure out the activity of participant, the teacher/trainer tells the participants that they can go up and join the participant by doing the same activity or adding on to it by connecting to the scene.

3. There should only be five participants up at a time.

VARIATIONS

1. The teacher/trainer can give the scene a theme or subject and ask the participants to connect the image to the theme or subject.

2. Create a more intimate and layered experience by having pair go up instead of a group.

10

Body Builders

Suggested Prop List
- ☒ Director's Slate
- ☐ Ball
- ☐ Construction Paper
- ☐ Dry Eraser Boards
- ☒ Colorful Scarves
- ☐ Pens, Pencils, Markers
- ☐ Play Microphone
- ☐ Other

BRAIN-BASED OBJECTIVES

To stimulate the senses

To grab participants' attention

To integrate physical activity

To invite choices and self-direction

GROUP SIZE

Two or more

SPACE REQUIREMENTS

Classroom size

TIME

10 to 20 minutes

FUNCTIONS

(Team Building, Communication Skills, Social Skills, Content Building, Critical Thinking Skills, Focus Activity)

PROCEDURE

1. The teacher/trainer tells the participants that he/she will call out an object and they are to form the object with their bodies.

2. First, the team members must discuss how they are going to create the object before the teacher/trainer tells them to start. Second, they can think in an abstract manner and use symbols to represent the word or theme.

3. This is effective when teams are in groups of three to five and they must come together and create the image with all of the team members in the group.

4. The teacher/trainer should then call out the same object, word, or theme to the group so that everyone must respond to the same information. Prepare yourself for different interpretations.

VARIATIONS

1. Give each team an index card with the name of the object and the other participants have to name the object.

2. This variation results in 100% non-verbal communication, which means absolutely no talking! The team members should follow the listed instructions found in the procedure section OR select one sculptor and their role is to have someone take the lead in creating the image.

11

Character Charades

BRAIN-BASED OBJECTIVES

To stimulate the senses

To grab participants' attention

To give the brain a break

To integrate physical activity

GROUP SIZE

Six or more

SPACE REQUIREMENTS

Classroom size

TIME

10 to 15 minutes

FUNCTIONS

(Team Building, Communication Skills, Social Skills, Content Building, Critical Thinking Skills, Focus Activity)

PROCEDURE

1. The teacher/trainer asks the participants to line-up into two different teams. He/she then tells them that as a whole team they will have to figure out the character that their teammate is trying to pantomime. The characters could be from a TV show or a movie, an animal, a music artist, or a famous figure.

2. The teacher/trainer should have the participants line-up and give numbers to each participant from each team in order to pair him or her up so they can compete. He/she should call one numbered pair up at a time. Once the pair is directly in front of the teacher/trainer they will receive a character to portray. Remember to whisper the name of the character so that distant team members do not overhear the selected character.

3. Once a teammate figures out the character, that is just the beginning because once the right character is called the teammate who pantomimed the character must run back and touch the hand of the teacher/trainer. Whoever touches the hand of the teacher/trainer receives the point.

VARIATIONS

1. Have the participants pantomime animals instead of characters for more physicality and creative thinking.

2. Give the individual a character card with a movie and ask the participant to pantomime a scene from the movie.

12

Grab-N-Go

BRAIN-BASED OBJECTIVES

To stimulate the senses

To invite choices and self-direction

To maximize feedback

To make learning rewarding

GROUP SIZE

Ten or more

SPACE REQUIREMENTS

Classroom size

TIME

10 to 15 minutes

FUNCTIONS

(Team Building, Communication Skills, Social Skills, Content Building, Critical Thinking Skills, Focus Activity)

PROCEDURE

1. The teacher/trainer has participants stand in two rows facing someone from the other team. He/she places an object such as an eraser or ball between the teams.

2. The teacher/trainer tells the participants that he/she will ask a question and the participant who thinks that he/she has the answer should run and try to grab the object to take it back home to their teammates. The participant must bring the object back to his/her teammate without being touched by someone from the other team.

3. If the teammate makes it back home with the object, he/she must consult with their teammates and then give the answer to the question. If the team answers incorrectly, the other team could decide to answer the question for the point or to pass. If they answer correctly, they will get the point and if they pass, the other team loses a point.

VARIATIONS

1. Give the participants a number and have them grab the eraser or ball when you call out their number.

2. Expand the first variation of Grab N' Go and allow each participant to link up with one or two of their team members. However, it has to be one of the members directly beside them and they must work as a unit to accomplish the goal and to secure a point.

13

Living Picture

Suggested Prop List
- ☒ Director's Slate
- ☐ Ball
- ☐ Construction Paper
- ☐ Dry Eraser Boards
- ☐ Colorful Scarves
- ☐ Pens, Pencils, Markers
- ☐ Play Microphone
- ☐ Other

BRAIN-BASED OBJECTIVES

To build a bridge to new learning

To engage emotional learning

To integrate physical activity

To invite choices and self-direction

GROUP SIZE

Two or more

SPACE REQUIREMENTS

Classroom size

TIME

10 to 20 minutes

FUNCTIONS

(Team Building, Social Skills, Content Building)

PROCEDURE

1. The teacher/trainer places participants into teams and tells them that he/she will give them a figure, shape, theme, or historical event to create with their bodies. The teams must discuss how they are going to create the image and what message they are trying to convey to the audience that will observe the "Living Picture."

2. The participants should give the image a slogan or a name and ask the viewers to share what they are trying to say about their group's image.

3. It is important to give enough time for each team to brainstorm so that they develop both the human image as well as the delivery of the message.

VARIATIONS

1. Have the participants bring the picture to life by adding a sound or actual dialogue that will elaborate on the selected image.

2. Select a passage from a mission statement, a current event, or a climax of a story and have them create a living picture. Then take a photograph of the team's image and add the written material to the picture that was based on the imagery work.

14

Meet and Greet

BRAIN-BASED OBJECTIVES

To reduce threat and stress

To find personal motivation

To grab participants' attention

To give the brain a break

GROUP SIZE

Six or more

SPACE REQUIREMENTS

Classroom size

TIME

30 to 45 minutes

FUNCTIONS

(Social Skills, Energizer)

PROCEDURE

1. The participants are to walk around the space and greet at least three people in the room. The greeting must be as dramatic as possible and

they both must give each other the best compliment they could ever imagine.

2. The teacher/trainer must emphasize the importance of accepting the positive compliment by providing a clear verbal response. For example, "thank you very much."

VARIATIONS

1. Have the participants meet someone new and introduce the person they met to the other group members.

2. Give the participants an index card that asks a question to get to know a person. The participants must meet and greet a participant and ask them the question on their card.

15

Scene Partner

Suggested Prop List

- ☒ Director's Slate
- ☐ Ball
- ☐ Construction Paper
- ☐ Dry Eraser Boards
- ☒ Colorful Scarves
- ☐ Pens, Pencils, Markers
- ☐ Play Microphone
- ☐ Other

BRAIN-BASED OBJECTIVES

To build a bridge to new learning

To enrich the learning environment

To engage emotional learning

To invite choices and self-direction

GROUP SIZE

Six or more

SPACE REQUIREMENTS

Classroom size

TIME

30 to 45 minutes

FUNCTIONS

(Social Skills, Content Building)

PROCEDURE

1. The teacher/trainer pairs up the learners and tells them that he/she will give them one of three genres: comedy, tragedy, or drama.

2. The teacher/trainer will give them a statement or issue and the participants must come up with a scene using the genre to share their opinion about the theme or designated topic.

3. Feel free to have participants add music to enhance their chosen genre.

4. Although optional, it is encouraging to have learners create a script before they present their scenes to ensure the flow and exchange of critical ideas and thoughts.

VARIATIONS

1. Have participants create scenes on video.

2. Solicit ideas and scenarios from participants and/or have them suggest questions, categories, or themes.

16

Stand in Line

BRAIN-BASED OBJECTIVES

To grab participants' attention

To give the brain a break

To integrate physical activity

To invite choices and self-direction

GROUP SIZE

Six or more

SPACE REQUIREMENTS

Classroom size

TIME

30 to 45 minutes

FUNCTIONS

(Team Building, Social Skills, Energizer, Focus Activity)

PROCEDURE

1. The teacher/trainer tells the participants that when he/she says, "stand in a line…" they should line up in the order of the statement. The statement could address an array of categorical concepts such

as alphabetical order based on first names, birth dates, shortest to tallest, length of hair, etc.

2. The teacher/trainer should give the participants 30 seconds to discuss and figure out how the line can form. Once they figure it out, the participants can discuss how they feel about their answers and what they learned about each other.

3. This engager can stand-alone. However, this can also be a great time to process what he/she experienced as the lines evolve and change based upon the statements that are placed on the floor.

VARIATIONS

1. Have the participants stand in line by specific groups or teams.

2. The participants can experience a deeper learning experience about a specific topic or procedure (great for reinforcement and review of working material and prior knowledge).

17

Team Back-to-Back

Suggested Prop List

- ☒ Director's Slate
- ☐ Ball
- ☐ Construction Paper
- ☒ Dry Eraser Boards
- ☒ Colorful Scarves
- ☒ Pens, Pencils, Markers
- ☐ Play Microphone
- ☐ Other

BRAIN-BASED OBJECTIVES

To build a bridge to new learning

To cultivate meaning

To engage emotional learning

To invite choices and self-direction

GROUP SIZE

Eight or more

SPACE REQUIREMENTS

Classroom size

TIME

10 to 20 minutes

FUNCTIONS

(Team Building, Communication Skills, Social Skills, Content Building, Critical Thinking Skills)

PROCEDURE

1. The teacher/trainer places participants into teams of four and have them decide who is going to be A, B, C, or D. The participants must decide in their group who is going to take on the role as director, actors, and writer.

2. The teacher/trainer tells the participants that they have to turn back-to-back, and once he/she says "Action" the teams must create a scene with a beginning, middle, and end with each participant playing his/her role.

3. The teacher/trainer can say "back-to-back" at any time to see how the team's process is developing. Once the engager is over, the writer must share the notes that the team came up with and the director should say 1,2,3, Action to share the scene.

VARIATIONS

1. Give teams a flipchart and designate participants to specific characters to develop a clear beginning, middle, and end. Then have them go back-to-back and then face-to-face to see how the two worlds' perspectives interact with one another. Then have the director record and/or recreate a scene.

2. Have teams create commercials to sell their point of view as it pertains to an objective or issue.

18

Team Groupings

Suggested Prop List

- ☐ Director's Slate
- ☐ Ball
- ☐ Construction Paper
- ☐ Dry Eraser Boards
- ☐ Colorful Scarves
- ☐ Pens, Pencils, Markers
- ☒ Play Microphone
- ☐ Other

BRAIN-BASED OBJECTIVES

To enrich the learning environment

To stimulate the senses

To grab participants' attention

To engage emotional learning

GROUP SIZE

Two or more

SPACE REQUIREMENTS

Classroom size

TIME

10 to 15 minutes

FUNCTIONS

(Team Building, Communication Skills, Social Skills, Critical Thinking Skills, Focus Activity)

PROCEDURE

1. The teacher/trainer gathers the participants to a space and tells them that he/she will come up with a category. Then the participants are to form groups according to the category.

2. Then the participants should be given time to discuss why they chose a certain group, and the teacher/trainer should select someone from the group to act as the reporter to share a statement.

3. The teacher/trainer can also use specific pedagogy that will enhance, review, or introduce a subject.

VARIATIONS

1. Have participants interview one another about the categories or theme.

2. Ask participants to form groups. discuss the content, and be able to record feedback to present to a larger group.

19

Team Storyboard

Suggested Prop List

- ☒ Director's Slate
- ☐ Ball
- ☐ Construction Paper
- ☐ Dry Eraser Boards
- ☒ Colorful Scarves
- ☐ Pens, Pencils, Markers
- ☐ Play Microphone
- ☐ Other

BRAIN-BASED OBJECTIVES

To build a bridge to new learning

To enrich the learning environment

To engage emotional learning

To invite choices and self-direction

GROUP SIZE

Six or more

SPACE REQUIREMENTS

Classroom size

TIME

30 to 45 minutes

FUNCTIONS

(Team Building, Social Skills)

PROCEDURE

1. The participants should divide into teams and create a sequence of three to five living pictures to tell the story of a theme, category, or content the teacher/trainer is trying to address. Make sure teams demonstrate a clear beginning, middle, and end.

2. Remember a living picture is a frozen picture (photo, painting, cartoon, or sculpture) that can serve to crystallize an idea or communicate a concrete image. These images may be sculpted into another image, brought to life, or captioned. A prime example is a newspaper photo accompanied by a headline.

3. Optional: Adding music to Team Storyboard is always an added feature with building both research and setting the tone for emotional engagement.

VARIATIONS

1. Allow the observers of the scene to freeze the action and give the characters other choices to make in the scene.

2. Videotape the scene and have the participants freeze the action on the tape and give feedback during playback mode. This gives you the freedom to stop it at anytime and discuss other aspects of the work, content, and character choices. For example, you can give descriptive and specifically provide feedback that speaks to the aesthetics, positions of the character's physical space, setting, review the role of power, and status.

20

Team Tapestry

Suggested Prop List

- ☐ Director's Slate
- ☐ Ball
- ☒ Construction Paper
- ☐ Dry Eraser Boards
- ☐ Colorful Scarves
- ☒ Pens, Pencils, Markers
- ☐ Play Microphone
- ☒ Magazine, glue

BRAIN-BASED OBJECTIVES

To cultivate meaning

To build a bridge to new learning

To engage emotional learning

To invite choices and self-direction

GROUP SIZE

Six or more

SPACE REQUIREMENTS

Classroom size

TIME

30 to 45 minutes

FUNCTIONS

(Team Building, Focus Activity, Social Skills)

PROCEDURE

1. The teacher/trainer places participants into teams and have them to cut out words or slogans from magazines that represent a specific subject, mission, and/or theme.

   Then they can glue or tape the words onto the construction paper in any type of format.

2. The teams must discuss their overall brain-based objectives for the tapestry and then choose those words and slogans that support their overall brain-based objectives.

3. Once the team is complete, the team should share the tapestry with the rest of the participants.

4. Since this is a group effort, it is helpful to place time constraints around this engager to keep everyone focused on the task and to build a sense of collaboration and completeness.

VARIATIONS

1. Have participants create individual life tapestries.

2. Ask each group to create a living picture, a commercial, or a scene advocating their preference.

21

Team Think-Link-Sync

Suggested Prop List

☐ Director's Slate
☐ Ball
☐ Construction Paper
☒ Dry Eraser Boards
☐ Colorful Scarves
☒ Pens, Pencils, Markers
☐ Play Microphone
☐ Other

BRAIN-BASED OBJECTIVES

To cultivate meaning

To build a bridge to new learning

To engage emotional learning

To invite choices and self-direction

GROUP SIZE

Six or more

SPACE REQUIREMENTS

Classroom size

TIME

10 to 20 minutes

FUNCTIONS

(Team Building, Communication Skills, Social Skills, Problem Solving, Content Building, Critical Thinking Skills)

PROCEDURE

1. The teacher/trainer asks participants to walk around the space and think to themselves or write on a topic or question provided by the teacher/trainer.

2. You should give the participants enough time to think or write, and then you can say "Link." Then, depending on how many team members the teacher/trainer says, the participants must link their arms around that many teammates.

3. The teams must now share their thoughts or ideas with their teammates. The teacher/trainer has the option to stop or continue the engager and have the participants link up with other teams or share with the rest of the class.

VARIATIONS

1. Ask participants to reflect on their experience, jot down key ideas, and then offer feedback to the class.

2. Have participants use cards and share their own choices.

22

Untangle

BRAIN-BASED OBJECTIVES

To stimulate the senses

To grab participants' attention

To give the brain a break

To integrate physical activity

GROUP SIZE

Five or more

SPACE REQUIREMENTS

Classroom size

TIME

10 to 20 minutes

FUNCTIONS

(Team Building, Social Skills, Critical Thinking Skills, Problem Solving, Focus Activity, Energizer)

PROCEDURE

1. Participants stand in a circle shoulder-to-shoulder putting their hands in the middle of the circle. After putting their hands in the middle, they must grab the hand of someone in the circle who is not next to them.

2. Once all of the hands join together and the participants are in a knot, the team must attempt to untangle themselves and try to get back to the original circle.

VARIATIONS

1. Divide your learners into two groups. Then ask the participants to compete with the other group(s), and the team that untangles first wins.

2. While standing shoulder-to-shoulder, have learners hold the hand with the person directly beside them then start to tangle the circle for about 30-45 seconds. Once "FREEZE" has been placed on the floor, everyone must stop and start to untangle, coming back to the neutral circle position. Raise the stakes by providing a time element to the untangling process.

Chapter Five

Engagers for Social and Emotional Skills

This next set of active strategies are geared towards the enhancement of social and emotional skills in your learners. Here, we provide a number of exercises, which will enhance, expand, and enlighten learners socially and emotionally.

You will find that some learners are advanced in terms of their ability to process logically instructional information but their capacity to connect and interact socially is underdeveloped. The creative techniques included in this segment represent just a few of our top engagers, which have proven to yield dramatic results, with tangible results regardless of the socio-emotional development level of the learner.

The suggested exercises in this chapter are designed to immediately grab the learners' attention and immerse them in the content. The scenarios simultaneously help develop the participants' interest to further academic growth. These activities each have an uncanny way of luring participants into the learning process while nurturing the socio-emotional realm—thereby yielding engaged, critical thinkers.

23

All Around the Room

BRAIN-BASED OBJECTIVES

To reduce threat and stress

To grab participants' attention

To give the brain a break

To integrate physical activity

GROUP SIZE

Six or more

SPACE REQUIREMENTS

Space to put chairs in a large circle

TIME

10 to 20 minutes

FUNCTIONS

(Energizer, Social Skills, Content Building, Focus Activity)

PROCEDURE

1. The teacher/trainer places chairs in a circle, and asks participants to sit in the chairs. There must be chairs for all of the participants in the

circle, and the teacher/trainer places himself/herself standing in the middle of the circle.

2. The teacher/trainer tells the participants that the person in the middle must say, "Move if ..." which tells us something about himself/herself. For example, "Move if you like pizza." If you are a classmate who likes pizza, you must get up and move to another chair. If he/she calls out, "all around the room," all of the participants must move to an empty chair.

3. It is important to note that the teammate who is left standing in the center becomes the person who calls out the next statement on the floor.

VARIATIONS

1. Have participants write out questions before the exercise and have participants move on the prepared questions.

2. Instead of chairs, you can have participants perform the exercise without chairs.

24

Back-to-Back

Suggested Prop List

☒ Director's Slate

☐ Ball

☐ Construction Paper

☐ Dry Eraser Boards

☒ Colorful Scarves

☐ Pens, Pencils, Markers

☐ Play Microphone

☐ Other

BRAIN-BASED OBJECTIVES

To engage emotional learning

To enrich the learning environment

To find personal motivation

To cultivate meaning

GROUP SIZE

Two or more

SPACE REQUIREMENTS

Classroom size

TIME

10 to 15 minutes

FUNCTIONS

Team Building, Energizer, Problem Solving, Social Skills, Content Building, Critical Thinking Skills, Focus Activity)

PROCEDURE

1. Participants are placed into pairs facing each other, and they decide who is going to be A or B. The teacher/trainer gives the participants a scenario to discuss.

2. The teacher/trainer tells the participants that they have to stand back to back. Once the teacher/trainer says 1, 2, 3, Action, the participants turnaround and face each other trying to solve the problem or discuss the scenario assigned. The teacher/trainer can say back to back at any time to have participants discuss where they are with the solution or how they are addressing the scenario.

VARIATIONS

1. If possible, form groups of three or four instead of pairs.

2. Have participants introduce their partners to the group.

25

Busy Highway

BRAIN-BASED OBJECTIVES

To reduce threat and stress

To enrich the classroom environment

To give the brain a break

To integrate physical activity

GROUP SIZE

Ten or more

SPACE REQUIREMENTS

Space to move around

TIME

10 to 20 minutes

FUNCTIONS

(Energizer, Social Skills, Focus Activity)

PROCEDURE

1. Participants divide into pairs. One must choose to be the car and the other to be the driver. The driver stands behind the car and places his/her fist in the middle of the car's back.

2. The participant who has chosen to be the car must close his/her eyes, and the driver guides them with their fist as the gearshift around the room. The middle of the back is STOP. The right shift is to turn toward the right, the left shift is to turn toward the left, and when the fist has the gear moving up and down it indicates to the driver move in that very direction (go up or go backwards).

3. The brain-based objective of this engager is for the driver to move through the highway without crashing into one of the other drivers and trust it can be done.

VARIATIONS

1. Select a participant to be an observer playing the role of a police officer or safety patrol. Ask them to give constructive and descriptive feedback on what they observed.

2. Create more obstacles by putting chairs in the space so that the participants have to maneuver more through the space.

26

Guess Who the Leader Is

BRAIN-BASED OBJECTIVES

To enrich the learning environment

To grab participants' attention

To give the brain a break

To integrate physical activity

GROUP SIZE

Six or more

SPACE REQUIREMENTS

Space to form a circle

TIME

10 to 20 minutes

FUNCTIONS

(Problem Solving, Social Skills)

PROCEDURE

1. The teacher/trainer asks one of the participants to leave the classroom so that he/she cannot see or hear. Once the participant is out, the teacher/trainer assigns someone to be the leader of a physical activity.

2. The other participants in the circle must copy the leader's activity without giving the leader away. Once the participants stand in the middle of the circle, the leader can change activities while the participant is trying to figure out who the leader is in that moment.

3. The participant standing in the middle of the circle could have up to three guesses depending on the size of the group.

VARIATIONS

1. Give the participant who will be leading the physical gestures a specific theme (representing key elements in a learning module, depicting specific task-related procedures) that is strictly content driven. The participant in the middle is not only identifying the leader now, but also identifying the learned concept and/or task.

2. Ask the leader of this engager if you can select two people to act as the leaders of the physical movements instead of one. However, the goal of the chosen leaders is to mirror one another without anyone suspecting that that is what is taking place.

27

Hear My Story, Tell My Story

Suggested Prop List

☐ Director's Slate
☐ Ball
☐ Construction Paper
☐ Dry Eraser Boards
☐ Colorful Scarves
☐ Pens, Pencils, Markers
☒ Play Microphone
☐ Other

BRAIN-BASED OBJECTIVES

To engage emotional learning

To enrich the classroom environment

To find personal motivation

To cultivate meaning

GROUP SIZE

Four or more

SPACE REQUIREMENTS

Classroom size

TIME

10 to 20 minutes

FUNCTIONS

(Social Skills, Communication Skills)

PROCEDURE

1. Participants work in pairs and tell the other participant a personal story. The story can be comic, dramatic, or tragic.

2. The other participant must physically tell the other participant's story to the other teammates through pantomime.

3. This can also be done with fiction and non-fiction literature as a way to review, introduce, or reflect on targeted information.

VARIATIONS

1. Have participants tell their story to a partner and then link up with another pair. After each person shares the person's story through pantomime and sound, the other pair must guess by sharing their interpretation of what they observed.

2. The second variation, which causes higher order and creative thinking, is to have the person share his/her story, whether comic, dramatic, or tragic, but this time by using his/her body and music or sounds (sounds are not words). Then his/her partner must write down and share what he/she observed to see how close he/she could get to what is being communicated.

28

Human Barometer

BRAIN-BASED OBJECTIVES

To build a bridge to new learning

To integrate physical activity

To invite choices and self-direction

To maximize feedback

GROUP SIZE

Ten or more

SPACE REQUIREMENTS

Classroom size

TIME

15 to 25 minutes

FUNCTIONS

(Problem Solving, Social Skills, Content Building, Critical Thinking Skills)

PROCEDURE

1. The teacher/trainer creates an imaginary line with one end starting at 0% and the other end at 100%. The teacher/trainer will give a statement

and the participants must place themselves according to their opinion on the barometer.

2. Once the participants align themselves, each of the groups must choose a spokesperson to discuss the topic. After the discussion, the spokesperson must present his/her point of view to the entire group.

3. After all of the groups share their points of view, the teacher/trainer can then ask if any of the participants were persuaded to move up or down on the barometer.

VARIATIONS

1. Have participants post notes on a flipchart and discuss the similarities and differences.

2. Present questions, concepts, or pieces of information covered in a previous session or class. Have participants vote on the one they want to review.

29

Inner and Outer Circle

BRAIN-BASED OBJECTIVES

To enrich the learning environment

To build a bridge to new learning

To invite choices and self-direction

To maximize feedback

GROUP SIZE

Ten or more

SPACE REQUIREMENTS

Space to make a circle

TIME

20 to 30 minutes

FUNCTIONS

(Social Skills, Content Building, Critical Thinking Skills)

PROCEDURE

1. Participants stand in two concentric circles, facing a partner. The inside circle faces out, the outside circle faces in. Participants ask questions of their partner or they may take turns responding to a teacher's/trainer's question(s).

2. Partners switch roles. Outside circle participants ask, listen, then praise or coach.

3. After each question or set of questions, participants in the outer or inner circle rotate to the next partner. (The teacher/trainer may call rotation numbers: "Rotate three ahead.")

VARIATIONS

1. Give participants a card with a question they have to answer from the content that you want them to learn. Then, have them ask the question on the card.

2. Have participants work on their listening skills by paraphrasing the statement of their partner.

30

Positive Corridor

BRAIN-BASED OBJECTIVES

To engage emotional learning

To reduce threat and stress

To enrich the classroom environment

To find personal motivation

GROUP SIZE

Ten or more

SPACE REQUIREMENTS

Space to move around

TIME

10 to 20 minutes

FUNCTIONS

(Social Skills, Focus Activity)

PROCEDURE

1. Participants must stand in two rows facing each other until they create to parallel lines with enough space for someone to walk. The key is to provide an illusion of a hallway corridor.

2. A selected teammate is charged with walking down the center of the corridor listening to the positive statements that their fellow teammates who are in the shape of a corridor will say to him/her.

3. It is easier to have one person from one side of the corridor to rotate turns and speak one at a time. Once the chosen teammate gets to the other end of the corridor, both teams would have had a chance to provide a positive response.

VARIATIONS

1. The first option is to use the engager of the corridor. However, a conflict must be identified and the person must slowly walk down the corridor listening to various solutions to the problem. By the time the learner arrives at the end of the corridor, he/she will have to conclude what he/she thinks was the most-effective solution and why.

2. This variation will allow your participants to practice a specific skill set or theory and/or to test out a standard. For example, review what it means to render good customer service and use a specific strategy with the difference being that while the participant is walking down the corridor, he/she must play the devil's advocate and think of an extremely disgruntled customer. The participant can stop at any time when one of the other participants has conveyed excellent and effective customer service (just think how many different scenarios you can place inside this engager).

31

Positive Push-Ups

BRAIN-BASED OBJECTIVES

To reduce threat and stress

To enrich the classroom environment

To find personal motivation

To grab participants' attention

GROUP SIZE

Six or more

SPACE REQUIREMENTS

Classroom size

TIME

10 to 20 minutes

FUNCTIONS

(Social Skills, Focus Activity)

PROCEDURE

1. The teacher/trainer asks one participant to leave the room or to stand out of earshot. When that participant is gone, the teacher/trainer requests that three or four participants make positive statements about the missing participant, including something special about that person's skills or achievements that not everyone might know.

2. The teacher/trainer can take on the role of a game show host on the show "Guess Who Said It." In the game show atmosphere, the host can ask for "upbeat, peppy, and positive words about your classmates." The trainer writes statements on the board.

3. When the participant comes back into the classroom, he/she tries to guess which one of his/her classmates made each statement. The participant has one chance to "Guess Who Said It." If he/she does not guess the right person, the participant who actually made the statement raises his/her hand.

VARIATIONS

1. Have the participants reverse roles to see things from a different perspective.

2. Have the person go through the same steps as listed in the Procedure section. However, after the person reveals the person who said the compliment, that person must offer that person a Positive Push-Up.

32

Spect-O-Gram

Suggested Prop List

- ☐ Director's Slate
- ☐ Ball
- ☒ Construction Paper
- ☐ Dry Eraser Boards
- ☐ Colorful Scarves
- ☒ Pens, Pencils, Markers
- ☒ Play Microphone
- ☐ Other

BRAIN-BASED OBJECTIVES

To build a bridge to new learning

To integrate physical activity

To invite choices and self-direction

To maximize feedback

GROUP SIZE

Six or more

SPACE REQUIREMENTS

Classroom size

TIME

10 to 20 minutes

FUNCTIONS

(Problem Solving, Social Skills, Content Building)

PROCEDURE

1. The teacher/trainer creates an imaginary line with one side labeled "Agree" and the other labeled "Disagree" and the center of the line labeled "Undecided." The teacher/trainer will give a statement and the participants must place themselves according to their opinion.

2. Once the participants align themselves, each of the groups must choose a spokesperson to discuss the topic. After the discussion, the spokesperson must present his/her point of view to the entire group.

3. After all of the groups share their points of view, the teacher/trainer can then ask if any of the participants were persuaded to move to another group.

VARIATIONS

1. Ask participants to raise both hands when they strongly agree with a response.

2. Ask participants to share as many solutions or answers as they can and add an element of time constraints.

Chapter Six

Engagers to Teach Content and Skills

Some experts believe that a subject is truly mastered only when a learner is able to teach it to someone else (Asian Proverb). The next grouping of strategies provide intensive methodologies for learning by examining specific information from varied perspectives. The seven exercises are taken from our assortment of noteworthy strategies that we have found to be the most rewarding in our instruction and training experience. These strategies facilitate the integration of difficult concepts and maximize meaning and analyses of the material.

The essence of these activities, which lead right into instruction and build skills, encourage brain stimulation and triggers prior knowledge. The exercises strengthen muscles in the brain to receive and store new thought patterns through the use of sensorial activity specifically, movement, sound, and rhythm. After engaging in some of these robust yet tangible ideas learners will be able to elicit new ideas, increase awareness and understanding of context, and foster critical thinking and creative thinking skills. These innovative strategies will promote group investment in learning and increase meta-cognitive analysis.

It is pertinent to be able to come up with new, innovative strategies that help you and your learners question, elicit answers based on content, and enable you to gain insight on how or what the mood, opinions, thoughts, and feelings are within the class.

33

Add-on-Story

Suggested Prop List

- ☐ Director's Slate
- ☐ Ball
- ☐ Construction Paper
- ☐ Dry Eraser Boards
- ☐ Colorful Scarves
- ☐ Pens, Pencils, Markers
- ☒ Play Microphone
- ☐ Other

BRAIN-BASED OBJECTIVES

To build a bridge to new learning

To reduce threat and stress

To enrich the learning environment

To engage emotional learning

GROUP SIZE

Six or more

SPACE REQUIREMENTS

Classroom size

TIME

10 to 20 minutes

FUNCTIONS

(Problem Solving, Social Skills, Communications, Critical Thinking Skills, Focus Activity)

PROCEDURE

1. The teacher/trainer has participants sit in a circle. The teacher/trainer can decide if she/he wants to start the story or end the story once that decision has been made. Then, you will let everyone know that each person will have about 30-45 seconds to add to the creation of a story. The teacher/trainer will state that the talking stick will go around the circle to each person after he/she claps his/her hands.

2. The handclap will act as a symbol for the talking stick to be passed to the next person, and then that person will add to the storyline wherever the person before them left off. The new person will pick-up where the story stopped.

3. Remember to emphasize the main parts of a story.

VARIATIONS

1. Ask participants to create a way to act out a concept without teacher/ trainer guidance.

2. Put props and items in the middle of the circle and have participants use the prop to add to the story.

34

Brainstorm A-Z

Suggested Prop List

☐ Director's Slate
☐ Ball
☐ Construction Paper
☒ Dry Eraser Boards
☐ Colorful Scarves
☒ Pens, Pencils, Markers
☒ Play Microphone
☐ Other

BRAIN-BASED OBJECTIVES

To build a bridge to new learning

To invite choices and self-direction

To maximize feedback

To make learning rewarding

GROUP SIZE

Four or more

SPACE REQUIREMENTS

Classroom size

TIME

15 to 25 minutes

FUNCTIONS

(Team Building, Social Skills, Content Building, Critical Thinking Skills)

PROCEDURE

1. Participants are placed into teams and given paper or dry eraser boards with the alphabets A-Z listed on it.

2. The teacher/trainer provides a theme, topic, or a question, and the participants are to come up with words that begin with the beginning of the listed alphabet they can think of for the topic.

3. The team that comes up with the most answers or finishes all of the alphabet letters first wins.

VARIATIONS

1. Instead of ending the activity with group discussions, create a panel or inner and outer circle (See dramatic engager # 29).

2. Pair up participants and have them play tic-tac-toe based on whether they can answer the review questions.

35

Commercial

Suggested Prop List

☒ Director's Slate
☐ Ball
☐ Construction Paper
☒ Dry Eraser Boards
☒ Colorful Scarves
☒ Pens, Pencils, Markers
☒ Play Microphone
☒ Other

BRAIN-BASED OBJECTIVES

To enrich the learning environment

To build a bridge to new learning

To invite choices and self-direction

To make learning rewarding

GROUP SIZE

Two or more

SPACE REQUIREMENTS

Classroom size

TIME

15 to 30 minutes

FUNCTIONS

(Team Building, Social Skills, Content Building, Critical Thinking Skills, Focus Activity)

PROCEDURE

1. Participants get with their team and discuss how they can create a 5-minute commercial to explain the topic that is given by the teacher/ trainer or a topic that they have chosen based on a subject, issue, or suggested theme.

2. The commercial must contain setlines, physical activity, a clear setting, clearly defined relationships between the characters, and portray a clear message.

3. Music, choreography, and props can be used to enhance the group's message.

VARIATIONS

1. Videotape the participants illustrating the concept and show it to the group.

2. Have participants do a mental imagery to visualize himself or herself or the situation.

36

Content Pantomime

BRAIN-BASED OBJECTIVES

To build a bridge to new learning

To enrich the learning environment

To integrate physical activity

To make learning rewarding

GROUP SIZE

Two or more

SPACE REQUIREMENTS

Classroom size

TIME

10 to 20 minutes

FUNCTIONS

(Critical Thinking Skills, Team Building, Social Skills, Content Building, Focus Activity)

PROCEDURE

1. Participants divide into teams, come up with symbols, and draw them on construction or poster board to represent the content provided by the teacher/trainer.

2. The teams are to present their symbols and/or representations based on interpretations of the content to the other class members.

3. Note that while one team is sharing their work, the other participants acting as the audience must copy the symbols that each group presents.

VARIATIONS

1. After the pair has completed their discussion or work, have them present or demonstrate before another pair of participants.

2. You can have participants write the scenes instead of having them present the scenes which reinforces their creative writing skills, and/ or record the story and present the playback to the group.

37

Jack-in-the-Box

BRAIN-BASED OBJECTIVES

To integrate physical activity

To invite choices and self-direction

To maximize feedback

To make learning rewarding

GROUP SIZE

Two or more

SPACE REQUIREMENTS

Classroom size

TIME

5 to 10 minutes

FUNCTIONS

(Social Skills, Content Building

PROCEDURE

1. Participants stand up from the chair if they have the answer to the question from the teacher/trainer.

2. The participant who stands up first gets to answer the question. If someone feels that the person answered incorrectly, he/she can stand up with his/her answer.

3. This can be done for a review, assessment, and/or to reinforce new information and skill sets.

VARIATIONS

1. Invite the participants to devise their own questions on the subject.

2. Have participants go around the room and have peers help answer questions that they don't know.

38

Learner-in-Role

Suggested Prop List

☒ Director's Slate
☐ Ball
☐ Construction Paper
☒ Dry Eraser Boards
☒ Colorful Scarves
☒ Pens, Pencils, Markers
☒ Play Microphone
☐ Other

BRAIN-BASED OBJECTIVES

To invite choices and self-direction

To find personal motivation

To engage emotional learning

To maximize feedback

GROUP SIZE

Three or more

SPACE REQUIREMENTS

Classroom size

TIME

15 to 25 minutes

FUNCTIONS

(Problem Solving, Social Skills, Content Building)

PROCEDURE

1. Participants take on expert roles given to them by the teacher/trainer. The roles could be doctors, lawyers, teachers, police officers, etc., and they are to challenge the teacher/trainer through the perspective of the assigned roles.

2. The objective is for learners to discover details about a character that the teacher/trainer is portraying. The learners-in-role interviews the individual and all of the inquiries may be made in a formal question-and-answer session format or improvisations.

3. It is set up in a formal format provide time for learners to research their roles and questions. If it is based on improvisation (to make it up on the spot), be prepared to go where they go and to use the devil's advocate strategy to deepen beliefs and to reiterate learning points.

VARIATIONS

1. Have the participants create a town meeting panel discussion and present their own views. Then, have other class members to speak.

2. Ask participants to prepare a case study for other group members.

39

Meet the Press

Suggested Prop List

- ☒ Director's Slate
- ☐ Ball
- ☐ Construction Paper
- ☒ Dry Eraser Boards
- ☒ Colorful Scarves
- ☒ Pens, Pencils, Markers
- ☒ Play Microphone
- ☐ Other

BRAIN-BASED OBJECTIVES

To build a bridge to new learning

To maximize feedback

To engage emotional learning

To invite choices and self-direction

GROUP SIZE

Four or more

SPACE REQUIREMENTS

Classroom size

TIME

10 to 20 minutes

FUNCTIONS

(Social Skills, Content Building, Communication)

PROCEDURE

1. The teacher/trainer divides the participants into teams and asks them to choose a person to be the reporter.

2. The team Brain-Based Objectives is to set up a press meeting, and the participants must write down questions they want to ask the reporter.

3. Once they have their questions, all learners role-play a mock press meeting individually asking their questions.

VARIATIONS

1. Pair up participants with different perspectives and ask them to compare their views. Alternatively, create a debate team with representatives from each perspective.

2. Have participants brainstorm a list, which could be relevant to the subject matter, job, or issue.

40

Pair Think-Link-Sync

Suggested Prop List

☐ Director's Slate
☐ Ball
☐ Construction Paper
☒ Dry Eraser Boards
☐ Colorful Scarves
☒ Pens, Pencils, Markers
☐ Play Microphone
☐ Other

BRAIN-BASED OBJECTIVES

To build a bridge to new learning

To maximize feedback

To engage emotional learning

To invite choices and self-direction

GROUP SIZE

Two or more

SPACE REQUIREMENTS

Classroom size

TIME

5 to 10 minutes

FUNCTIONS

(Critical Thinking Skills, Problem Solving, Social Skills, Content Building)

PROCEDURE

1. The teacher/trainer asks the participants to walk around the space and think to themselves or write on a topic or question provided by the teacher/trainers.

2. You should give the participant enough time to think or write and then you can say "Link," and whoever the participant is next to he/she must link their arm around that person to make him/her a partner.

3. The pairs must now share their thoughts or ideas with their partner. The teacher/trainer has the option to stop or continue the engager and have participants link up with other pairs or share with rest of the class.

VARIATIONS

1. Pair up participants, have them interview each other, and poll the entire group to obtain the results.

2. Ask participants to locate someone who is different from them.

41

Pair Walk-and-Talk

Suggested Prop List

- ☐ Director's Slate
- ☐ Ball
- ☐ Construction Paper
- ☒ Dry Eraser Boards
- ☐ Colorful Scarves
- ☒ Pens, Pencils, Markers
- ☐ Play Microphone
- ☐ Other

BRAIN-BASED OBJECTIVES

To build a bridge to new learning

To invite choices and self-direction

To make learning rewarding

To maximize feedback

GROUP SIZE

Two or more

SPACE REQUIREMENTS

Classroom size

TIME

5 to 10 minutes

FUNCTIONS

(Problem Solving, Social Skills, Content Building)

PROCEDURE

1. All learners are asked to get their journals and to write out their thoughts, feelings, opinions, and/or questions on the topic or content provided by the teacher/trainer.

2. Then the participants are asked to stand up and get into pairs. Once the pairs have been identified, then they will be instructed to walk around the room discussing their journal entries.

3. The last step here is for the participants to go back to their journals and to create a list about the pro's and con's/similarities and differences that they observed during their walk and talk with their partner.

VARIATIONS

1. Create different roles and ask participants to create questions that test participants' understanding of the material.

2. Ask participants to find another participant and found out how many matches can be made with another person.

42

Role on the Board

Suggested Prop List

- ☐ Director's Slate
- ☐ Ball
- ☒ Construction Paper
- ☐ Dry Eraser Boards
- ☐ Colorful Scarves
- ☒ Pens, Pencils, Markers
- ☐ Play Microphone
- ☐ Other

BRAIN-BASED OBJECTIVES

To build a bridge to new learning

To engage emotional learning

To give the brain a break

To invite choices and self-direction

GROUP SIZE

Four or more

SPACE REQUIREMENTS

Classroom size

TIME

10 to 20 minutes

FUNCTIONS

(Social Skills, Content Building)

PROCEDURE

1. The teacher/trainer will draw an outline of a figure on the board or smart board as an outline of a figure of a human body.

2. All learners are asked to think of an image of a character. Then they are asked to fill-in the diagram by brainstorming the strengths, weaknesses, characteristics, appearances, identifying hopes and fears, and listing the many roles the selected character may have to play in society or has played in an assigned story or module.

3. As an option, you can have everyone create one role on the wall or have a figure and have him or her work individually as they build their character's information.

4. Once the information is written into the drawing of the figure, create a name for this role or identify the role that was predetermined by the teacher/trainer.

VARIATIONS

1. Instead of a flipchart, have participants create a "shield" or "coat of arms" that demonstrates their goals and accomplishments.

2. Have participants create a personal self-assessment instead of creating a public exercise.

43

Star Witness

Suggested Prop List

- ☒ Director's Slate
- ☐ Ball
- ☐ Construction Paper
- ☒ Dry Eraser Boards
- ☒ Colorful Scarves
- ☒ Pens, Pencils, Markers
- ☒ Play Microphone
- ☐ Other

BRAIN-BASED OBJECTIVES

To build a bridge to new learning

To engage emotional learning

To invite choices and self-direction

To maximize feedback

GROUP SIZE

Four or more

SPACE REQUIREMENTS

Classroom size

TIME

10 to 20 minutes

FUNCTIONS

(Social Skills, Content Building, Critical Thinking Skills, Communication Skills)

PROCEDURE

1. The teacher/trainer places the participants in teams and ask them to choose a star witness.

2. The teacher/trainer informs the team to set up a court setting, and the participants must write down questions they want to ask the witness.

3. After writing down their questions, the participants get to ask the witness their individual questions.

VARIATIONS

1. Send participants' ideas to extend their learning for a few weeks after the session is over.

2. Have the scene videotaped. Then, play back and discuss with the participants alternative ways to solve the issue.

44

Teacher-in-Role

BRAIN-BASED OBJECTIVES

To build a bridge to new learning

To engage emotional learning

To invite choices and self-direction

To maximize feedback

GROUP SIZE

Six or more

Space Requirements:

Classroom size

TIME

15 to 25 minutes

FUNCTIONS

(Communication Skills, Social Skills, Content Building, Critical Thinking Skills)

PROCEDURE

1. The teacher/trainer plays the role of a character who the participants must ask questions or challenge.

2. Remember to use props and the scarves in any way you choose to help deepen the believability of the chosen character.

3. Note: A teacher-in-role is a demonstration of an individual who interacts with the participants (audience members) takes on a role that might control the action, excite interest, invite involvement, provoke tension, challenge thinking, create choices and ambiguities, or further develop the narrative (Rjinbout, 1995).

VARIATIONS

1. Invite the participants to make you the Jack-in-the-Box from their questions.

2. Instead of having a group discussion, divide the participants into trios. Assign one of the participants to a trio group, and then ask each group to give the assigned participant supportive feedback.

45

Word Ball

Suggested Prop List
- ☐ Director's Slate
- ☒ Ball
- ☐ Construction Paper
- ☐ Dry Eraser Boards
- ☐ Colorful Scarves
- ☐ Pens, Pencils, Markers
- ☐ Play Microphone
- ☐ Other

BRAIN-BASED OBJECTIVES

To make learning rewarding

To enrich the learning environment

To maximize feedback

To invite choices and self-direction

GROUP SIZE

Three or more

SPACE REQUIREMENTS

Classroom size

TIME

10 to 15 minutes

FUNCTIONS

(Social Skills, Content Building, Critical Thinking Skills)

PROCEDURE

1. Participants are divided into teams and asked to review the content by tossing the ball to one another.

2. The objective of this engager is to get as many people around the circle to share and express themselves based on the given topic. The tossing of the ball enables the person to say ONE WORD.

3. The teacher/trainer states that the key to the tossing is to throw it under handed at all times (this cuts down on odd throwing abilities and increases catching chances). You may want to say, "This ball represents the pulse of our group/ community, and, therefore, it is important that we tap into the heart of who we are and how we think, while thinking about keeping the beat of our collective heart alive."

4. After the teacher/trainer says places the theme or subject that is being reviewed, the team provides a one-word response by tossing the ball while saying the answer. This can be used as a vocabulary review or simply to go over procedures and/or assess where the group is as an opener or as a closure.

VARIATIONS

1. Use the engager to test if the participant can perform a skill instead of a knowledge question.

2. Prepare an observer feedback sheet to share views and perspectives, topic, scene, or subject matter.

Chapter Seven

Engagers for Review and Reinforcement

One of the most effective ways to build knowledge, skills, attitude, and behavior is taking the time to assess and perform evaluations. In this section, we offer several unique techniques that are flexible enough to support diverse subject areas. The line of exercise will act as a major alternative to the standard pen and paper assessments and evaluations. Each strategy was selected and devised in a format that will help maximize the benefits of assessing anywhere from group dynamics, to academic levels in terms of cognition and recognition, to a classroom's attitude and behavior as well as learning styles on both an individual or group level.

All of the active exercises will enable the educator or facilitator to generate group gaps, group solutions, and identify prior knowledge, progression of new material, and the retention of critical information. As you consider which strategies and specific exercises that are most appropriate for your active learning environment, note that these series of assessment and evaluation activities were designed and suggested based on two different academic and social emotional perspectives.

One perspective allows you to learn about the deficits and progression based on skill development. Skills include technical and non-technical skill sets. You will assess and evaluate where each learner is, how much they have developed, and how best to further practices when working with them and others in the future. The second perspective allows one to examine and empathize with the learner's feeling, values, and attitudes. In summary, this chapter provides opportunities to increase the use of creative assessment and evaluation options, supports monitoring and tracking of both participant and information, and creates a space for recognition of completion.

46

Four Corners

Suggested Prop List

☐ Director's Slate
☐ Ball
☐ Construction Paper
☒ Dry Eraser Boards
☐ Colorful Scarves
☒ Pens, Pencils, Markers
☐ Play Microphone
☐ Other

BRAIN-BASED OBJECTIVES

To make learning rewarding

To build a bridge to new learning

To invite choices and self-direction

To maximize feedback

GROUP SIZE

Three or more

SPACE REQUIREMENTS

Classroom size

TIME

10 to 15 minutes

FUNCTIONS

(Social Skills, Content Building)

PROCEDURE

1. The teacher/trainer informs participants that the room will be turned into a game board. The teacher/trainer says, "Each corner of the room represents A, B, C, and D answers." Therefore, the questions should be structured into the format of inventory, review, quiz, or test questions.

2. Team members are asked to write answers down on their dry eraser boards. Emphasize to work individually first, then come together to exchange answers.

3. Once the teacher/trainer asks the question all learners respond in the order set in Step 2. Then once the group collaborates and agrees on what they think the right answer is, one person moves to one of the four corners of the room.

4. It is important that the recorder of each reports their answer by standing in one of the four corners. If it's the right answer, they get a point. If it's the wrong answer, they must go back and discuss what they missed. If they are able to explain on the dry eraser board why they changed their answer and the rationale is incorrect, they receive a point. This is a WIN/WIN ENGAGER.

VARIATIONS

1. Ask participants to stand up or line up in order of how much they agree with a statement.

2. Have participants to interview classmates whose answer or ranking is different from their own.

47

Grab-N-Review

Suggested Prop List

- ☐ Director's Slate
- ☒ Ball
- ☐ Construction Paper
- ☒ Dry Eraser Boards
- ☐ Colorful Scarves
- ☒ Pens, Pencils, Markers
- ☐ Play Microphone
- ☐ Other

BRAIN-BASED OBJECTIVES

To integrate physical activity

To invite choices and self-direction

To maximize feedback

To make learning rewarding

GROUP SIZE

Ten or more

SPACE REQUIREMENTS

Classroom size

TIME

10 to 15 minutes

FUNCTIONS

(Team Building, Communication Skills, Social Skills, Content Building, Critical Thinking Skills, Focus Activity)

PROCEDURE

1. The teacher/trainer has participants stand in two rows facing someone from the other team. He/she places an object such as an eraser or ball between the teams.

2. The teacher/trainer tells the participants that he/she will ask a question and the participant who thinks they have the answer should run and try to grab the object to take it back to their teammates. The participant must bring the object back home to his/her teammates without being touched by someone from the other team.

3. If the teammate makes it back home with the object, he/she must consult with their teammates and then give the answer to the question. If the team answers incorrectly, the other team could then decide to answer the question for the point or to pass. If they answer correctly, they will receive the point and if they pass, the other team loses a point.

VARIATIONS

1. Create a flipchart to display on the wall so that participants can refer to the answers through the session.

2. Invite the participants to select their own questions to ask the participants.

48

Review A-Z

Suggested Prop List

- ☐ Director's Slate
- ☐ Ball
- ☒ Construction Paper
- ☒ Dry Eraser Boards
- ☐ Colorful Scarves
- ☒ Pens, Pencils, Markers
- ☐ Play Microphone
- ☐ Other

BRAIN-BASED OBJECTIVES

To build a bridge to new learning

To invite choices and self-direction

To maximize feedback

To make learning rewarding

GROUP SIZE

Three or more

SPACE REQUIREMENTS

Classroom size

TIME

10 to 15 minutes

FUNCTIONS

(Social Skills, Content Building)

PROCEDURE

1. The teacher/trainer must place a question that reviews or reinforces new information that has been shared over a period of time.

2. Participants are placed into teams and given paper or dry eraser boards with the alphabets A-Z.

3. The teacher/trainer gives a topic or question to review, and the participants are asked to come up with words that begin with as many alphabet letters they can think of for the topic.

4. The team that comes up with the most answers or finishes are the winners. All answers must relate to content area.

VARIATIONS

1. Have the participants choose a theme from their list and create a living picture from their words.

2. Instead of a living picture, you can have the pictures create a scene that captures their words.

49

Review Barometer

BRAIN-BASED OBJECTIVES

To make learning rewarding

To build a bridge to new learning

To invite choices and self-direction

To maximize feedback

GROUP SIZE

Four or more

SPACE REQUIREMENTS

Classroom size

TIME

10 to 20 minutes

FUNCTIONS

(Social Skills, Content Building)

PROCEDURE

1. The teacher/trainer creates an imaginary line with one end starting at 0% and the other end at 100%. The teacher/trainer will give a statement

and the participants must place themselves according to the certainty of their answer to the question on the barometer.

2. Once the participants align themselves each of the groups, they must choose a spokesperson to discuss their answer. After the discussion, the spokesperson must present his/her point of view to the entire group.

3. After all of the groups share their points of view, the teacher/trainer can then ask if any of the participants were persuaded to move up or down on the barometer.

VARIATIONS

1. Have participants create a panel of video reviewers.

2. Have participants write final thoughts on a flipchart taped on the wall.

50

Review Toss

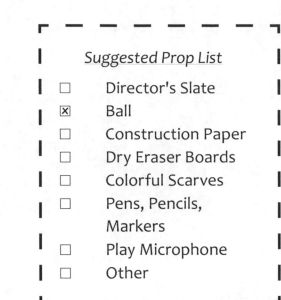

Suggested Prop List

- ☐ Director's Slate
- ☒ Ball
- ☐ Construction Paper
- ☐ Dry Eraser Boards
- ☐ Colorful Scarves
- ☐ Pens, Pencils, Markers
- ☐ Play Microphone
- ☐ Other

BRAIN-BASED OBJECTIVES

To make learning rewarding

To enrich the learning environment

To maximize feedback

To invite choices and self-direction

GROUP SIZE

Three or more

SPACE REQUIREMENTS

Classroom size

TIME

10 to 15 minutes

FUNCTIONS

(Social Skills, Content Building)

PROCEDURE

1. Participants are divided into teams and asked to review the content by tossing the ball to one another.

2. The objective of this engager is to get as many people around the circle to share and express themselves based on the given topic. The tossing of the ball enables the person to say ONE WORD.

3. The teacher/trainer states that the key to the tossing is to throw it under handed at all times (this cuts down on odd throwing abilities and increases catching chances). You may want to say, "This ball represents the pulse of our group/ community, and therefore, it is important that we tap into the heart of who we are, and how we think while thinking about keeping the beat of our collective heart alive."

4. After the teacher/trainer places the theme or subject that is being reviewed, the team provides a one-word response by tossing the ball while saying the answer. This can be used as a vocabulary review or simply to go over procedures and/or assess where the group is as an opener or closure.

VARIATIONS

1. Ask participants to express appreciation to the person who tossed him or her the ball.

2. Instead of a ball, toss yarn or another object. As each person receives the object, he/she can express his/her feelings, thoughts, and opinions.

References

Adams, K. (2005). *The sources of creativity and innovation* [Commissioned Paper]. Retrieved July 12, 2014, from: http://www.fpspi.org/pdf/innovcreativity.pdf

Brain Facts and Figures [Database record]. (2014). Retrieved March 11, 2014, from: http://faculty.washington.edu/chudler/facts.html#brain

Basom, J. (2006). *Drama games: Powerful pedagogy for the 21st century classroom.* AATE Conference. Lecture conducted from Convention Center, Washington, DC.

Bolton, G. (1979). *Towards a theory of drama in education.* London: Longman.

Cook, H.C. (1917). *The play way.* New York, NY: Frederick A. Stokes Co.

Franken, R.E. (1994). *Human motivation* (3rd ed.). Belmont, CA: Brooks/Cole Publishing Co.

Gallien, L.B., Jr., and Peterson, M.S. (2005). *Instructing and mentoring the African-American college student: Strategies for success in higher education.* Boston, MA: Pearson Education, Inc.

Gardner, H. (2000). *Frames of mind: The theory of multiple intelligences for the twenty-first century.* New York, NY: Basic Books.

Goleman, D. (1995). *Emotional intelligence: Why it can matter more than IQ* (2nd ed.). New York, NY: Bantam Books.

Goleman, D. (2006). *Social intelligence: The revolutionary new science of human relationships* (2nd ed.). New York, NY: Bantam Books.

Heathcote, D., & Bolton, G. (1995). *Drama for learning: Dorothy Heathcote's mantle of the expert approach to education.* Portsmouth, NH: Heinemann.

Jensen, E. (2005). *Teaching with the brain in mind.* (2nd Ed.). Association for Supervision and Curriculum Development, Alexandria: Va.

Jensen, E. (2008). *Brain-based learning: The new paradigm of teaching.* Thousand Oaks, CA: Corwin Press.

Johnson, A.P. (1998). How to use creative dramatics in the classroom. *Childhood Education,* 75 (1), 2-9.

Kelly, M. Understanding and using learning styles [About.com: Secondary Education commentary] Retrieved July 8, 2014, from: https://712educators.com/od/learningstyles/a/learning_styles.htm

Kuh, G.D. (2001). *Assessing what matters to student learning: Inside the national center for student engagement.* Journal Article [*Change*] 33 (3) 10-17.

Kuh, G.D. (2013). What matters to student success: the promise of high-impact promise. Retrieved June 2014 from the National Institute for Student Learning Outcomes Assessment website https://www.learningoutcomesassessment.org

Koziol, S.M., Jr., & Richards, L.A. (1996). *Basic informal drama exercises for active learning in the primary classroom: A practical handbook.* Sarajeva, Bosnia UNICEF.

Lee, C.D., & Smagorinsky, P. (2000). *Vygotskian perspectives on literacy research:* Constructing meaning through collaborative inquiry. Cambridge, England: Cambridge University Press.

Levy, J. (1987). *A theatre of the imagination.* Charlottesville, VA: New Plays Inc.

Lightman, A., Attention and the brain. The New Yorker Magazine, October 1, 2014. Retrieved from: www.newyorker.com/tech/elements/anatomy-attention on October 4th 2014

McClasin, N. (1990). *Creative drama in the classroom.* (5th)ed.). Studio City, CA: Players Press, Inc.

Nachmanovitch, S. (1990). Free play. New York, NY: St. Martin's Press.

O'Neil, C. (1995). *Drama worlds: A framework for process drama.* Portsmouth, NH: Heinemann.

Oriental Outpost: Adventures in Asian Art [eCommerce] Retrieved May 23, 2014, from: http://www.orientaloutpost.com/shufa. php?q=when+three+people+gather+one+becomes+a+teacher

Rijnbout, F. (1995). *Creative dramatics in the classroom.* New York University Seminar. Lecture conducted from NYU. New York, NY.

Rodriquez, C. [Camille Rodriquez]. (2010, January 26, 2010). Active reading - the first step in the learning process [Blog post]. Retrieved August 19, 2014, from: http://ezinearticles.com/?Active-Reading---The-First-Step-in-the-Learning-Process&id=3643237

Rogers, E. (August 2003). Diffusion of innovations. (5th ed.). Free Press.

Rusbult, C. [Craig Rusbult]. (2002). Strategies and motives for personal education [Blog post]. Retrieved August 12, 2014, from: American Scientific Affiliation website: http://www.asa3.org/ASA/education/learn/motives. htm

Rusbult, C. (Ed.) Active-learning theories. Retrieved August 12, 2014, from: http://www.asa3.org/ASA/education/teach/active.htm

Salovey, P., & Mayer, J.D. (1990). *Emotional intelligence.* New Haven, CT: Baywood Publishing.

Settles, B. (2010). *Active learning literature survey (1648).* Retrieved from burrsettles website: http://burrsettles.com/pub/settles.activelearning.pdf

Smilkstein, R. (2011). We're born to learn. (2nd ed.). Thousand Oaks, CA: Corwin Press.

Smith, B.L., & MacGregor, J.T. (1992). *What is collaborative learning?* State College, PA: National Center on Postsecondary Teaching, Learning, and Assessment at Pennsylvania State University.

Sternberg, R.J. (Ed.). (October 1997). Intelligence and lifelong learning. *American Psychologist, 52.* Retrieved from: http://www.apa.org/pubs/journals/special/4015210.aspx

University of Maine Center for Inclusion & Disability Studies (2011). Friends and feelings: Social emotional-development in young children in growing ideas toolkit. Retrieved May 28, 2014, from: https://ccids.umaine.edu/files/2014/02/social-emotional-tip-022714.pdf

Wagner, B.J. (1976). *Dorothy Heathcote: Drama as a learning medium.* Washington, DC: National Educational Association.

Wagner, B.J. (1991) Imaginative Expression. In *Handbook of Research on Teaching The English Language Arts* (2nd ed.), 2003. Mahwah, NJ: Lawrence Erlbaum Associates.

Ward, W. (1930). *Creative Dramatics.* New York, NY: Appleton-Century.

Ward, W. (1957). *Playmaking in education with junior school children.* Prentice Hall, Inc., p. 14.

Way, B. (1967). *Development through drama.* London: Longman.

Wenger, E. (1998). *Communities of Practice Learning, Meaning, and Identity.* New York, NY: Cambridge University Press.

Willis, J. (2007). *Brain-based learning: Strategies for improving student's memory, learning, and test-taking success* [Journal Article]. Childhood Education 83 (9).

Willis, J.A. (Spring 2006). Research-Based Teaching Strategies for Improving Learning Success. California Association of Independent Schools (CAIS) Faculty Newsletter.

Willis, J. (July 27, 2012). A neuroscientist makes the case for teaching teachers about the brain [Online Forum Commentary] Retrieved August 2, 2014, from:https://www.edutopia.org/blog/neuroscience-higher-ed-judy-willis

Zins, J.E., Weissberg, R.P., Wang, M.C., & Walberg, H.J. (2004). *Building academic success on social and emotional learning.* New York, NY: Teachers College Press.